The Other Book

Waid-Sainvil

TOB - This book is dedicated to my brother, Jesus Zamora.

To Jesus Zamora, my brother dear,
This book is yours, with gratitude sincere.
Your help and guidance, treasured and profound,
In every line and chapter, your support is found.

My love for you is vast, my thanks unbound,
Your dedication and commitment are renowned.
In every challenge faced, your presence shines,
A testament to loyalty that intertwines.

Your role has been pivotal, your impact clear,
In our shared success, you're ever near.
Your efforts have shaped this journey's course,
A meaningful force, a guiding source.

With heartfelt thanks, this tribute I convey,
For all you've done, in every way.
Your support means more than words can say,
In every page, your essence will stay.

TABLE OF CONTENTS

TOB

PREFACE

TOB - Commonly known as The Theory of the Body, it introduces fresh perspectives on faith, drawing from religious teachings. It reorganizes ancient beliefs into a cohesive narrative of salvation history, illustrating how vocational life connects to this overarching story.

This framework provides a new language and structure for exploring fundamental questions about human existence. It addresses the reasons for our creation and outlines our life's purpose, inviting deep reflection on these essential topics.

My book also uses the acronym TOB, which stands for The Other Book\Teachings Of Billy. This title follows my first work, WOW (Word Of Waid), maintaining a thematic link between them. Like the first, TOB is inspired by the Teachings Of Billy, also with the acronym TOB.

The principles discussed in this book are rooted in the Creation Energy Teachings, which serve as a foundation for understanding our existence. These teachings guide individuals toward a greater awareness of their roles in the world.

The book aims to help readers become their truest selves, promoting a life of peace and harmony. It emphasizes the importance of inner tranquility and positive relationships with others as essential components of fulfillment.

By recognizing their true essence, individuals can appreciate their place in the larger mosaic of life. This understanding leads to a more genuine existence characterized by universal love and compassion.

Although the insights in this book are articulated through my voice, they are deeply influenced by the teachings of Billy Meier. This connection enriches the content and roots it in a broader spiritual tradition.

TOB serves as a source of inspiration, encouraging readers to embark on their personal journeys of growth. Through exploration and self-reflection, individuals can discover deeper meanings and align with universal truths.

Ultimately, the goal of TOB is to illuminate paths toward a harmonious life. By engaging with these teachings, readers can embrace love and purpose as guiding principles in their lives.

In conclusion, TOB is designed to provoke thought and encourage introspection. It highlights the significance of living in alignment with universal values, fostering transformation and growth throughout the journey of life.

The Heart's Depths

From the depths of consciousness, thoughts take flight,

Giving rise to feelings that shape day and night.

These emotions weave together our inner design,

Guiding our character, our virtues entwined.

To forge our identity, we must heed the call,

Embracing the laws that govern us all.

In following creation's wise, gentle sway,

We nurture our spirits, finding our way.

Through reflection and effort, our essence unfolds,

In harmony with nature, our true story told.

Each guideline a beacon, illuminating the path,

Leading us closer to wisdom's sweet aftermath.

So let us embrace this journey with care,

As we cultivate ourselves, each moment we share.

For in the heart's depths, a profound truth lies,

A testament to life where our spirit will rise.

THE NEW AGE

In our youth of understanding,
Potential vast begins to gleam,
Physical mastery strides boldly,
Yet, puzzles linger in the dream.
The New Age whispers mysteries,
Infancy of knowing's sway,
Beyond mere flesh and solid grasp,
True mastery awaits the day.

THE PATH TO VIRTUE

The powers arise through life's vibrant breath,

Yet virtues must blossom from struggles, not death.

In harmony with creation's guiding hand,

We cultivate goodness as we learn to stand.

To integrate fully with laws that inspire,

We weave our intentions with a creative fire.

In wise, thoughtful action, we find our true way,

Embracing responsibility in each passing day.

For the path to virtue demands our own toil,

A commitment to nurture through sweat and through soil.

In the dance of existence, we forge our own light,

Guided by wisdom, we rise to new heights.

So let each endeavor reflect our intent,

As we strive for the virtues that life has sent.

In this sacred pursuit, we honor the call,

For within us resides the potential of all.

JMMANUEL

In ages past, Jmmanuel's quest,

Truth bearer, noble, and blessed.

His words, unwritten, left to fade,

Misshapen by time's relentless blade.

Two millennia swept away,

Creation's essence, finding its way.

Now Billy Meier, his spirit renewed,

Guides with wisdom, eternal and true.

GALLERY OF LIFE

In the grand gallery of life, we're each a lens,
Capturing moments as the world unfolds, transcends.
Through these eyes, diverse perspectives bloom,
A mosaic of stories, casting light in every room.
Sharing our visions, expanding what we know,
In each perspective, a new dimension to grow.
No singular viewpoint holds the whole truth,
Together, our rainbow sparks a vibrant youth.
Let's treasure the richness in our varied view,
Painting the tapestry of human breakthrough.
In unity, we forge connections strong and clear,
Bridging divides, finding common ground sincere.
With open hearts and minds, we stand aligned,
In the harmony of our collective design.
Dreaming of a world where peace finds its way,
Where empathy and understanding lead each day.

SELF-COMPASSION

Each person must show kindness to the soul,

Embrace the love that dwells inside,

For self-compassion forms the base,

Where true acceptance can abide.

With honesty, confront your thoughts,

Explore your feelings, deep and clear,

Understanding breeds a stronger self,

Creating safety year by year.

Let openness guide your heart's intent,

And trust the emotions that arise,

In every action and quiet choice,

Find the truth that never lies.

So cherish the warmth you seek within,

In nurturing love, let your spirit rise,

For in the journey of knowing self,

You'll discover the light that never dies.

CAUSE AND EFFECT

Through every age and realm, cause and effect entwine,

A cosmic dance that spans both space and time.

From the genesis of stars to the galaxies' expanse,

Their intertwined embrace, in eternal trance.

Across the voids where universes unfold,

Their echo resounds, a tale yet untold.

In each fleeting moment and celestial arc,

Cause births effect, igniting the spark.

Through dimensions vast, beyond mortal ken,

Their symphony plays again and again.

In the pulse of creation, from dawn to twilight,

Cause shapes destiny in its celestial flight.

From the birth of a universe to its fading glow,

Cause and effect in relentless flow.

Threads of existence, woven and spun,

In the web of time, their dance is never done.

In the silence of stars and the chaos of birth,

Cause and effect shape the cosmos' mirth.

In every corner where life may be found,

Their presence profound, forever profound.

FROM AGES LONG PAST

All that we inherit from ages long past,
Echoes of lives where memories are cast,
In joys and in sorrows, in lessons, we find,
A wealth of experience shaping the mind.
Through countless existences, we carry the weight,
Of wisdom accumulated, of fate intertwined,
Not buried in shadows of the subconscious deep,
But in memory banks where, our essence will keep.
Each moment we cherish, each truth we have known,
Forms a mosaic vibrant, uniquely our own,
From the pages of history, our spirits arise,
With the stories of lifetimes beneath endless skies.
As we navigate life's ever-changing embrace,
We draw from these echoes, each memory a place,
For every experience, both bitter and sweet,
Crafts the journey of being, making us whole and complete.

Moment's Dance

In every moment's dance, pursue peace's tune,

Let harmony weave through morning, night, and noon.

A tranquil journey etched by hearts attune,

Where respect blooms freely 'neath the sun and moon.

Let voices ring out, diverse and unconfined,

In equality's cradle, let understanding find.

Each viewpoint honored, like pearls in the tide,

In life's grand fabric, let harmony abide.

EARTHLY ARROGANCE

Earthly arrogance, boundless and vast,

Dictates how others must think and feel,

Yet each soul, unique, walks its own path,

Living, loving, as its own will.

To demand conformity is to deny,

The essence of individuality's grace,

For in diversity, humanity thrives,

Each heart a symphony in its own space.

APOPHIS

In the velvet expanse where stars bind,

Comes Apophis, a fleeting sign,

On Friday the 13th, in twenty-twenty-nine's glow,

Earth gazes up, watching its cosmic show.

No fear grips hearts, for Earth shall abide,

Spared from the meteor's fiery ride,

Seven years pass, Apophis returns anew,

Earth's people wiser, with lessons true.

A farewell whispers through the starry dome,

As an old friend and planet find their home,

In the dance of cosmos, a gentle decree,

Earth bids adieu with grace and reverie.

In The Garden Of Souls

In the garden of souls, let kindness bloom,
As petals of empathy unfurl in place,
Each heart a mirror, reflecting in tune,
The golden rule, a timeless embrace.
With gentle hands and words that mend,
We paint the canvas of life's shared art,
In every gesture, a message to send,
A symphony of love from the heart.
For in the quiet moments we connect,
In the language of compassion's song,
Each act of kindness, a sweet dialect,
Where harmony and empathy belong.
So let us nurture this sacred ground,
Where respect and understanding thrive,
In every soul, a bond is found,
Treat others well, and love will revive.

Cause Births Effect

Through every age and realm, cause and effect entwine,
A cosmic dance that spans both space and time.
From the genesis of stars to the galaxies' expanse,
Their intertwined embrace, in eternal trance.
Across the voids where universes unfold,
Their echo resounds, a tale yet untold.
In each fleeting moment and celestial arc,
Cause births effect, igniting the spark.
Through dimensions vast, beyond mortal ken,
Their symphony plays, again and again.
In the pulse of creation, from dawn to twilight,
Cause shapes destiny, in its celestial flight.
From the birth of a universe to its fading glow,
Cause and effect in relentless flow.
Threads of existence, woven and spun,
In the web of time, their dance is never done.
In the silence of stars and the chaos of birth,
Cause and effect shape the cosmos' mirth.
In every corner where life may be found,
Their presence profound, forever profound.

LET YOUR SPIRIT FLY

When truth feels heavy, burdening your core,
It's like descending into a chasm's floor.
The spirit's teachings, met with pain and strife,
Can cast a shadow on the light of life.
But when you choose to welcome what is real,
A ladder rises, guiding how you feel.
Each step ascends, revealing truths so bright,
As signs of hope emerge to fill the night.
The power is yours, to sink or to climb,
To dwell in darkness or embrace the rhyme.
With knowledge lighting pathways, love can bloom,
And harmony dispels the shadows' gloom.
For within your heart lies freedom and peace,
A journey of the soul that will not cease.
So choose with courage, let your spirit fly,
Into the vast expanse of the open sky.

Past Lives Fade

Past lives fade, their tales untold,
No more their nature, no more their hold.
Focus now on the life you live,
Each moment a gift, each choice to give.
In this existence, growth finds its seed,
Fulfillment blooms from every deed.
Wisdom gathered from lives gone by,
In your subconscious, it does lie.

TEACHING OF LIFE

In life's rich fabric, teachings abound,

From the mundane to profound, they resound.

Called the Teachings of Life, a timeless name,

Every interaction, a lesson to claim.

With rocks and trees, creatures, and kin,

Each encounter holds wisdom within.

Moments unfold, revealing their lore,

A boundless wellspring of ideas galore.

From everyday scenes to moments profound,

Life's teachings echo, endlessly profound.

In Ancient Texts

In ancient texts, the tale is spun,
Of sorrow's rise when all begun,
Prophet Henoch speaks of the fall,
Semjasa's name echoes through it all.
From the Lyra's depths, they came to roam,
Nagal's legacy, a shattered home,
With Nakar's worlds in ruin and strife,
Their actions shaped the course of life.
As leaders clashed, Semjasa and foe,
Nuclear fires lit the earth below,
A cycle of chaos, destruction unfurled,
Leaving shadows across the world.
Yet from despair, a promise arose,
Through countless lives, their purpose grows,
Transforming hearts, they strive to mend,
Healing the past, as time begins to bend.

120 BILLION

In realms unseen, where spirits soar,

120 billion, forevermore,

Linked in We-form, they intertwine,

In cosmic dance, beyond confines of time.

Their consciousness, many of them, a higher plane,

Yet to return, from where they came,

No heaven's gate, no fiery pit,

Just universal consciousness, infinite.

Creation's hand, the guiding thread,

Weaves through galaxies, where truth is spread,

No heaven's heights, no depths of hell,

Just cosmic order, where all dwell.

In this grand design, we find our place,

Among the stars, in cosmic grace,

120 billion spirits shine,

Linked to the Universe divine.

OMELETTE

To craft an omelette, eggs must break,
Shells shattered, their essence awake.
From fragility springs culinary grace,
Yolk and white merge, a savory embrace.
Each crack, a sacrifice for the plate,
Whisked with care, ingredients innate.
Transformation sizzles, a symphony's call,
Eggs broken, nourishing one and all.
In simplicity rests this truth so profound,
To birth creation, shells must unbound.
Omelette born from the breaking of dawn,
An ode to beginnings, in every morn.

Prophet Jeremiah

In ancient times, the prophet Jeremiah spoke,
A man would come, his words a cloak,
With universal truths to share,
A guiding light for all to bear.
His message spread, igniting minds,
Yet ancient sects, with wary signs,
Would rise in shadow, push against,
As history's cycles reoffend.
The spirit's wisdom, rich and deep,
In every heart, its promise seeped,
A vision bright, uniting lives,
In harmony, the spirit thrives.
Through the years, acceptance grew,
Reincarnation's essence, too,
Embraced by faiths both old and wise,
A new dawn breaks, as truth will rise.

TRUE LOVE

In the realm where Earth bound hearts entwine,

We yearn for true love's essence divine.

Beyond the grasp of mortal coil,

A love eternal, beyond turmoil,

Secrets whisper where hearts align,

In timeless dance, souls intertwine.

There, bathed in purest, sacred light,

True love blooms, infinite & bright.

No Savior But Ourselves

No savior comes to lift our plight,
No external force to guide our flight,
Yet in this truth, a marvel springs,
We wield within vast, potent wings.
For we, each one, with boundless might,
Hold keys to realms of infinite light,
In love's grip and wisdom's lore,
Creation's wonders evermore.
Each breath a hymn to cosmic dance,
Each thought a seed of circumstance,
In every soul we meet and greet,
The universe's heartbeat.
With love and kindness as our creed,
We journey forth, fulfill our need,
To glimpse the grandeur, vast and true,
In every moment, life anew.

Harness Our Thoughts

Thought is the mightiest force, a powerful stream,

The essence of existence, the heart of our dream.

It is thought, energy and vibration combined,

The fundamental cause of all that we find.

In the sphere of our lives, each moment and choice,

Thoughts shape our reality, giving us voice;

From ideas that spark to the actions we take,

The world is influenced by the paths that we make.

As causative forces weave through our day,

They guide our intentions, lighting the way;

In this intricate dance of creation and fate,

Our thoughts are the seeds that determine our state.

So let us wield this power with wisdom and care,

For in every thought lies potential to share;

In the vastness of existence, let clarity reign,

As we harness our thoughts, let love be our gain.

Blood Clot

In the island breeze once flowed,

Words "blood clot" in the Jamaican tongue,

Now tainted by a new disease,

COVID's shadow, where hope once sung.

Vaccines promised shield and might,

Yet inefficiency unveiled their plight,

Families weep, loved ones part,

In the grasp of a pandemic's dark.

From households echoed cries of pain,

Where once joy and laughter reigned,

Now death's cold hand claims its due,

As COVID's toll, relentless, accrues.

Blood clot, once a phrase benign,

Now echoes loss in whispered rhyme,

A world transformed by unseen foe,

Leaves hearts heavy, with sorrow's woe.

Dance Of Delight

The spirit form endures, yet ever it grows,

Increasing in power, as wisdom bestows.

Unchanged in its essence, it flourishes bright,

Gathering knowledge, embracing the light.

In realms of the spirit, it journeys afar,

Evolving through cycles, guided by stars.

Each sojourn in purity enriches the soul,

Preparing for rebirth, to play a new role.

With every return, the spirit takes flight,

Reborn in the body, a dance of delight.

Alongside the consciousness, a new self takes shape,

Transforming its essence, as boundaries escape.

Together, they rise, in unity's grace,

Crafting new pathways as time leaves its trace.

For in every rebirth, the spirit's embrace,

Is a journey of growth in the vastness of space.

THE CREATORS

Through the Creational law of interaction, we see,

All phenomena woven in unity;

A seamless thread connects each life and thought,

In this grand tapestry, our truths are sought.

If we doubt our capacity to truly thrive,

We give life to the doubt, letting it drive;

But in every moment, we hold the command,

At the helm of our journey, we choose where we stand.

We can lead with intention or drift with dismay,

Navigating the currents of thought every day;

In harnessing our power, we shape what we find,

For the mind is a vessel, guided by design.

So let us seize the potential we hold,

Choosing to flourish, letting our stories unfold;

In the interplay of all that we are,

We create our own futures, and shine like a star.

EARTH DWELLERS

Earth's dwellers, in their mundane stride,

Life's true essence often denied.

Yet deep within, Creation's fire,

Guides souls higher, ever higher.

Through cycles spun, in mortal frame,

Evolution's dance, no two the same.

Till souls transcend the human plight,

To realms where life's true meanings alight.

OPINION

In minds' kaleidoscope they bloom,

Opinions, varied as the moon.

Each soul, a voice, distinct and bright,

In the symphony of thought's delight.

Like stars that dot the endless sky,

Opinions gleam, they amplify.

For every soul beneath the sun,

A thought, a tale, unique, undone.

In Future Times

In future times, when dreams take flight,
Humans will traverse the endless night,
Conquering the void, reaching far and wide,
Exploring the cosmos with hearts as their guide.
They'll forge great stations beyond the air,
Where countless lives will gather and share,
In bustling realms where work takes form,
Creating a future both bold and warm.
With each new journey, horizons expand,
As they uncover wonders across the land,
Together they'll reach for stars above,
Bound by a vision of unity and love.
In these distant days, the universe vast,
Humanity's spirit will soar at last,
Crafting a legacy among the skies,
With hope and courage, they'll rise and rise.

THE RHYTHM OF LOVE

Nothing surpasses love; it reigns supreme,

The essence of understanding, the heart of our dream;

It transcends the confines of time's fleeting flow,

A force that existed before beginnings could grow.

Beyond any ending, love's light will endure,

An endless continuum, profound and pure;

We are all part of this vibrant embrace,

Connected in harmony, sharing one space.

When we recognize this truth and align our way,

Life transforms into a magnificent display;

In each moment of kindness, in every shared smile,

We celebrate existence, each heartbeat worthwhile.

So let love guide us, in all that we do,

For in its warm glow, we find strength anew;

In the grand tapestry of life's endless song,

Love is the rhythm to which we all belong.

HUMAN SKILL

In the quiet depths where thoughts reside,

Lies a power waiting to be untied.

Free will, a gift unknown, unseen,

A force that shapes each life's scene.

Teach not this essence, for it must be found,

Through journeys deep, where silence abounds.

Human hearts hold this precious key,

To choose their path, to set thoughts free.

Within the realm of mind's domain,

Lies the potential to break every chain.

Thoughts, like seeds in fertile ground,

Grow into actions profound.

Discover this truth, let it unfold,

A story of courage, of mysteries untold.

For in the dance of thought and will,

Lies the essence of human skill.

In This Realm

In the realm where Earth bound hearts entwine,

We yearn for true love's essence divine.

Beyond the grasp of mortal coil,

A love eternal, beyond turmoil,

Secrets whisper where hearts align,

In timeless dance, souls intertwine.

There, bathed in purest, sacred light,

True love blooms, infinite & bright.

FRAGILE EARTH

Upon this fragile Earth we tread,

Seeking peace where shadows spread,

Yearning for calm amidst the strife,

Yet silence eludes, the tumult rife.

Wings outstretched, the eagle soars,

In search of heights where dreams ignite,

Yearning to dominate the skies,

But destiny waits as daylight dies.

Two wings that carry ambition high,

Across the vast expanse of time and space,

Shaping a world with resolute pace,

Hegemony's call, an endless chase.

The eagle's flight, a ballet in the air,

A symphony of strength and dare,

However, touched by the sun's warm kiss,

It descends humbled, yearning for bliss.

Then, in the quiet of its grounded stance,

Amidst the ashes of its fiery dance,

Peace may dawn upon this Earth's domain,

As wings of power yield to a serene refrain.

GILGAMESH

In the cradle of time,

Gilgamesh did roam,

A shape-shifting soul far from his home.

120,000 years his lifespan once knew,

Now reduced to 50,000, as Earth's hue.

He molded his being to fit this new land,

Internally and externally, he did expand.

No beamship could return him whence he came,

For his planet was lost in a cosmic flame.

Gilgamesh, last of his kind, lingers here alone,

In a world that's now his eternal home.

THE DANCE

Dance your dance, unbound and free,

In the music's embrace, let your spirit be.

Feel the rhythm, the pulse, the beat,

In every step, find joy so sweet.

No need to conform, just move with grace,

Let your body express in its own unique pace.

For in the sway of each graceful prance,

You find yourself in the dance.

The music whispers, the heart replies,

As you twirl beneath the open skies.

Embrace the moment, let worries fade,

In this dance of life, find serenade.

With every sway, every gentle sway,

Let the music guide you, come what may.

So dance your dance with love and light,

In the rhythm of joy, make your flight.

Dance Of Creation

No one thinks our thoughts; the power is ours,

We shape our own minds, guiding our stars;

Responsible for ourselves in every way,

We hold the key to each moment and day.

When we embrace the truth of our might,

Living in harmony, we ignite the light;

With knowledge as our guide, we find the way,

And the Universe responds to the paths we lay.

In helping ourselves, we unlock the door,

To abundance and growth, to what we explore;

The energy we summon flows back in kind,

As the cosmos aligns with the strength of our mind.

So let us be mindful of the thoughts that we weave,

For everything shifts with the dreams we believe;

In this dance of creation, let purpose prevail,

As we harness our power, we truly set sail.

In Silence

As I evolve, reverence blooms anew,

For choices made, beliefs embraced,

In the dance of life, perspectives accrue,

The more I grow, humility seized.

Silent echoes of acceptance ring,

Amidst the chorus of diverse voices,

In understanding, wisdom springs,

In silence, my Spirit rejoices.

NOKODEMION

In realms of half-material light,

Where Creation's mysteries ignite,

Nokodemion soared to greater heights,

Truth's harbinger in cosmic nights.

Nine-point-six billion years in flow,

Oldest spirit, Earthly ebb and glow,

Prophets' voices through ages told,

Galileo, Socrates of old.

Aristotle's wisdom, Rasputin's might,

Mozart's melodies in starlit flight,

From Henock to Jmmanuel,

Mohammed's grace,

In prophets' forms, his timeless face.

Billy, his seventh reign,

Guides humanity through trials and pain,

Till 3999, his path unfurled,

To lead us to the cosmic world.

WEB OF CREATION

Creation is not bound by dark or light alone,

But framed by constants, in a realm of its own;

Laws that govern the dance of thought and deed,

Where actions echo, and intentions take seed.

When we align with these principles clear,

The effects we encounter draw ever near;

For every cause holds a promise profound,

In the fabric of existence, our choices are found.

This intricate balance shapes all that we see,

In the web of Creation, we're part of the key;

By honoring the laws that guide our way,

We harness the power of each dawning day.

So let us act wisely, with purpose and care,

In the harmony of existence, let love be our prayer;

For in following truth, we unlock the design,

In the heart of Creation, our destinies align.

THE DESTROYER

The Destroyer Planet, banished far and wide,

By Plejaren hands, across the cosmic tide.

Ancestors' folly let it breach our domain,

Now gone, may Earth forever remain.

No fear of its return, no havoc it shall sow,

Safe in our skies, where peaceful breezes blow.

Guarded by time's gate, our world's serene track,

The Destroyer's tale, never to circle back.

MALONA

In distant world where Sirius gleams,

Malona met its shattered dreams.

Warriors of gene-manipulated hand,

Tore apart their verdant land.

Phaeton, once a planet bold,

In fiery depths its story told.

Ocean's fury met volcanic might,

Sundering Malona's celestial light.

Now the Asteroid Belt, a cosmic tomb,

Holds fragments of Malona's doom.

Mars now orbits where once it lay,

A dance of planets in disarray.

Sirius, distant, silent and grand,

Watches as history shifts like sand.

Malona's legacy, a celestial art,

In fractured echoes, tells its part.

DYNAMIC FLOW

The mentality shapes not just what we do,

But draws in the world, crafting paths anew;

Thoughts are hyper frequencies, swift and bright,

Radiating outward, igniting the night.

These energies flow, an electromagnetic dance,

Connecting with echoes that spark and enhance;

As we live and learn, our minds weave a stream,

Creating vast currents from each vivid dream.

In this dynamic flow, our thoughts intertwine,

Gathering strength, as intentions align;

Enormous waves of energy pulse and blend,

Molding our reality, shaping each trend.

So let us be mindful of the thoughts that we send,

For they shape our experience, our lives they transcend;

In the vastness of being, let love be the core,

Attracting abundance, opening every door.

THE LOGIC OF LOVE

Love is logic, a profound refrain,

A frequency woven through time's endless chain;

It deepens and evolves, a force ever strong,

Binding us together, where we all belong.

In this vast expanse, everything aligns,

On an infinite spectrum, where connection shines;

Multidimensional threads weave worlds far and wide,

In galaxies and clusters, love is our guide.

Across cosmic networks, where stars gently gleam,

Each heartbeat echoes, a shared, vibrant dream;

In the dance of existence, all souls intertwine,

In the embrace of the universe, love's essence will shine.

So let us awaken to this truth we hold dear,

In the logic of love, let go of all fear;

For in every moment, across time and space,

Love's frequency resonates, uniting our race.

HEAL

When love's path diverges, and parting draws near,
Take not their choice as a wound to fear.
Each heart beats with its own unique song,
With reasons and yearnings, where they belong.
Instead of dwelling on what could not be,
Embrace their decision, let your spirit free.
Respect their autonomy, their right to choose,
Grant them the grace, their path to pursue.
Forcing affection against their will,
Only brings pain that love cannot heal.

Toxic Energy

In hearts where anger and envy reside,
Where jealousy and resentment collide,
With vengeance and rage, a turbulent blend,
Unhappiness brews without an end.
These emotions cloud judgment's view,
Tainting interactions, casting a hue,
Of dissatisfaction and discontent,
Spreading negativity wherever they're sent.
To protect your well-being, heed this call,
From those whose toxic energy may fall,
Boundaries are crucial, set them strong,
To keep your peace where you belong.
Their influence can darken your light,
Affecting your mood day and night,
Stay mindful, guard your positivity,
In the face of their stormy activity.
For happiness thrives in a clear, open space,
Where toxic emotions find no place,
Choose peace and joy, let negativity part,
And embrace the serenity within your heart.

THE EGO

The ego "I" must harness reason's might,

Let intellect illuminate the way,

Demand the best from deep within,

And shape your path with choice each day.

With clarity as your guiding star,

Forge a life that reflects your will,

In harmony with your own true self,

Pursue the goals that inspire and thrill.

So cultivate a life of thought and care,

Obey the voice that's wise and free,

For in this quest for inner truth,

You'll find your purpose, bold and serene.

HONESTY

In the dance of shared reality, truth must flow,

Honesty and transparency, seeds we sow.

Speaking openly, minds clear and true,

Creates paths for understanding to ensue.

Authenticity, a beacon bright and clear,

Guides us past misunderstandings, near and dear.

THE TEACHINGS

In the universe of Creation's Energy Teachings,
A profound journey awaits those seeking meanings.
Embracing principles with wholehearted trust,
Heeding recommendations, pathways adjust.
Delving deeper into wisdom's embrace,
A transformative shift finds its place.
Events align, seemingly destined to be,
Unfolding miracles, astonishing to see.
In this realm where possibilities unfold,
The extraordinary becomes the norm, bold.
Awe and wonder stir at creation's art,
Revealing a world where dreams depart.
In its embrace, trust and respect ignite,
Nurturing relationships, strong and right.

PERFECT IMPERFECTION

Each person must face their truest self,

Acknowledging flaws that shape their way,

For no one dwells in a world of perfection,

Mistakes and lessons guide each day.

We're bound to stumble on this path,

Learning and growing through each fall,

For clarity is seldom found,

And none can claim they know it all.

In the tapestry of human hearts,

Imperfection is a common thread,

No one is better, no one is less,

In this shared journey, all are led.

So embrace your nature, flawed and real,

With humility, let compassion grow,

For in accepting ourselves as we are,

We find the grace that helps us glow.

The pulse and the rhyme

Within each heart, a spark awaits,

A power longing to be set free,

It calls to us, to nurture our fates,

To let our spirits grow, endlessly.

In thoughts that wander and dreams that soar,

New capabilities emerge with time,

Discoveries waiting on the edge of the door,

Each insight a rhythm, a pulse, a rhyme.

Embrace the journey, let questions ignite,

For in the search, our true selves align.

Through challenges faced and wisdom in sight,

We forge our paths, our spirits entwined.

So let your gifts expand, reach out and climb,

In the dance of creation, let visions arise.

For in the hands of humankind, in each moment and time,

Lies the power to shape futures, where potential lies.

THE CALL

Across epochs summoned, humanity hears,

Echoes of a message through time's ancient spheres.

Deep within our souls, let it imprint its mark,

A beacon of light in the eternal dark.

Tethered to infinity, through lifetimes we've tread,

Countless futures beckon, paths yet to be led.

Embrace this awareness, our interconnected fate,

Weaving as one, in the tapestry we create.

Unified in essence, bound as a race,

Embracing our truth with steadfast grace.

Humanity's journey, a collective quest,

In unity we thrive, in unity we rest.

Kelch Der Wahrheit

In centuries vast, eight hundred years ahead,

A shift shall blossom where our spirits tread.

With hearts united, peace will find its place,

As truth awakens in the human race.

The winds of change will whisper through the night,

And guide us toward a future bathed in light.

Yet all must strive to turn the wheel just right,

For harmony requires our shared insight.

The book, "Kelch der Wahrheit," bears the key,

Its pages rich with wisdom, clear and free.

As seekers delve into its sacred text,

A path unfolds, transforming hearts perplexed.

Together we will nurture seeds of grace,

And cultivate a world where love will trace.

Through truth's embrace, our spirits will ascend,

In unity, we forge a brighter end.

Ego Awaken

In the depths of mind, ego awakes,

Through subconscious realms, connections make.

Overall Consciousness Block, where wisdom gleams,

Awakens the self from dormant dreams.

Material and subconscious merge as one,

Liberating the spirit, the journey begun.

Self-awareness blooms, autonomy found,

In the union of mind, profound and profound.

THE GREAT EMBRACE

We must embrace our true self,

A leader born from within the heart,

With visions clear, and dreams to weave,

We chart a course, we play our part.

Ideas spark like stars in night's expanse,

Nurtured by passion, we take ourr flight,

In pursuit of goals, relentless and bold,

Transforming thoughts into action's light.

So rise with purpose, let your voice be heard,

Forge paths anew with courage and grace,

For in the dance of self-discovery,

Your unique leadership finds its place.

COMPETITION

Competition's shadow darkens the way,

Dividing hearts, where harmony should sway.

In its midst, individuals clash and contend,

Resentment grows, a bitter trend.

Children taught to excel, to outpace,

Miss the beauty of a collaborative embrace.

Anxiety and stress, their constant foes,

As comparison's burden only grows.

Let us nurture unity, let cooperation bloom,

In collective effort, dispel competition's gloom.

For a society to thrive, in peace's domain,

Cooperation and harmony must reign.

FORGIVING

To forgive is to find peace deep within,

Letting go of resentment, where healing begins.

Not excusing the hurt, nor forgetting the past,

But choosing to release, free from bitterness amassed.

Reclaiming your power, taking hold of your fate,

Choosing forgiveness, no longer to hate.

Breaking the cycle of anger and pain,

Opening up to liberation, a new path to gain.

For holding onto grudges, bitterness thrives,

Forgiveness breaks chains, where tranquility thrives.

In forgiving those who've caused you pain,

Inner peace blossoms, like gentle rain.

SUCCESS

One's triumph rings through the collective soul,

A testament to unity's steadfast goal.

In shared success, each heart finds its role,

A harmonious chorus where aspirations extol.

No solitary victory, but a communal rise,

Where one's achievement lifts all to the skies.

Bound by bonds of solidarity, strong and true,

Together we flourish, in everything we pursue.

Your Attitude

In your demeanor, your essence shines bright,

A mirror reflecting your inner light.

Attitude speaks of the soul within,

A portrait painted by the spirit's spin.

Not just a mask, but a true reflection,

Of thoughts and beliefs, a deep connection.

In words and deeds, it boldly tells,

The story of who within you dwells.

So let it be true, let it be kind,

Your attitude, the voice of your mind.

In its grace and strength, let it define,

The beauty and depth of your design.

Dear Mom

Dear Mom, in love's purest, I hold you dear,

I've witnessed your sacrifices, felt every tear.

Your strength and love have shaped our way,

Guiding us, your children, through each night and day.

You've raised us well, with wisdom, fully.

Your time on Earth, a cherished memory.

Now, as you journey homeward bound,

Your spirit echoes, a beautiful sound.

In our hearts, you forever reside,

Your legacy of love, our eternal guide.

Until we meet again, beyond life's bend,

Your soul, dear Mom, we'll always defend.

LOGIC

Where logic's insights and visions spread.

Foreseeing predictions in wisdom's flight,

They journey forth in knowledge's might.

Their minds entwined with scholarly grace,

Exploring depths in the learning's embrace.

Each revelation a beacon, a guide,

As they navigate life's intricate tide.

In the realm where intellect and intuition meet,

They decipher truths, both bitter and sweet.

Through teachings bound, their spirits ignite,

In pursuit of understanding's pure light.

UNDERSTANDING

In the depths of understanding, silence reigns,

Wisdom's gentle whispers, no need for strains.

As knowledge grows, words gently fade,

In quiet contemplation, truths cascade.

The more you grasp, the quieter you stay,

In silent knowing, thoughts find their way.

Reflections deepen, in tranquil retreat,

Understanding unfolds, calm and complete.

In stillness, wisdom's essence is found,

Where silence speaks, profound and profound.

The more you comprehend, the less you speak,

In peaceful understanding, serenity seeks.

THE SELF

Fear no one, but yourself, beware,
Where dwells the main enemy, so rare.
In the depths within, where shadows creep,
Confront thyself, where secrets keep.
No foe compares to doubts and fears,
Where inner battles stir, unseen tears.
The self, the adversary in the dark,
Where courage falters, leaving a mark.
Conquer the fears that within reside,
The true enemy, where doubts abide.
In self-awareness, find strength untold,
Fear no one but yourself, be bold.

In The Whispers Of Thoughts

In the whispers of thoughts that quietly roam,

Reach out to those who make your heart home.

For in this vast world, connections weave,

Unseen ties that in our souls cleave.

Feel the presence of kindred spirits near,

In the silent dialogue that's always clear.

Through these invisible threads that bind,

We're united beyond space and time.

Connect with hearts you hold in thought,

In the realm where unseen currents wrought.

For we're all part of this cosmic thread,

Touching lives, where love is spread.

I Love You

Always leave loved ones with "I love you,"
A phrase that lingers, tender and true.
In fleeting moments, before you part,
Let these words echo, from heart to heart.
For life's journey is brief, time slips away,
Express your love, come what may.
In every farewell, let affection bloom,
"I love you," a melody that dispels gloom.
In these simple words, a bond is sealed,
Hearts warmed, wounds healed.
So before the day is through,
Always leave loved ones with
"I love you."

THOUGHTS OF GOODNESS

When thoughts of goodness fill your mind,

Embrace them well, let actions flow,

For from kind seeds, true value grows,

In gentle deeds, their worth will show.

Nurture the feelings that uplift,

Transform the light within your heart,

For when you share your brightest gifts,

You spark the change, you play your part.

So let your visions take their flight,

With purpose clear, let passion guide,

In every step, create with love,

For in these acts, true treasures bide.

SPEAK TRUTH

Speak truth with every breath you take,

In honesty, let your heart be found,

Affirm only what you know to be,

For in this light, true wisdom's bound.

Let words be anchored, clear and strong,

In certainty, let your voice arise,

For empty claims can lead us wrong,

And shadows linger where doubt lies.

So choose your words with thoughtful care,

In every truth, let trust be sown,

For speaking clear and standing bare,

Builds bridges where we're not alone.

SADNESS

Sadness through hurts, a paradoxical sway,

Unbalances the psyche in its own strange way.

Emotions entwine in a tangled weave,

Where pain's embrace oddly relieves.

In the depths of sorrow, a peculiar solace lies,

Unveiling truths beneath tear-filled skies.

The mind shifts, unsettled and unsure,

Navigating emotions that obscure.

Yet within this turmoil, a strange comfort blooms,

A nuanced understanding in grief's dark rooms.

For sadness, though painful, can also reveal,

Hidden depths of the heart, raw and real.

ONENESS

A time will come when hearts unite,

Humanity forged in shared insight,

Each life a piece of the greater plan,

Together we rise, hand in hand.

No more divided by skin or creed,

But bound by the truths that we all need,

In the light of creation's guiding hand,

We'll understand where we all stand.

Our strength lies not in differences shown,

But in the common ground we've grown,

Embracing the laws that bind us tight,

Illuminating paths with shared light.

So let us walk this journey bold,

In unity's warmth, let love unfold,

For in our oneness, we truly thrive,

Connected in spirit, fully alive.

CHANGING DAYS

On Earth, a realization dawns,

To re-evaluate truths we've drawn.

Our knowledge rests on beliefs deep-rooted,

Yet many are flawed, misconstrued.

These convictions shaped by biased eyes,

Misinformation veils the skies.

To progress, we must unlearn,

Critically examine and discern.

Dismantle the old, question anew,

Let go of what we thought we knew.

Expand our minds, break through the haze,

Embrace growth in these changing days.

THE PROPHETS' WHISPERS

In time, the Earth will lend its ear,

To prophets' whispers, wise and clear,

A chorus rising from the ground,

Where truth and understanding are found.

With open hearts, they'll learn to see,

The ties that bind humanity,

Each voice a thread, each word a light,

Illuminating shadows of night.

For when one suffers, all shall feel,

The weight of pain, the wounds that heal,

In empathy, their spirits blend,

A world transformed, where love transcends.

Thus, hand in hand, they'll walk the way,

Embracing dawn of a brighter day,

Together in a sacred trust,

United, rising from the dust.

Mutual Embrace

A woman is not mere property to possess,

Her needs and desires must be met with respect.

True connection arises from mutual intent,

In the space where both hearts willingly intersect.

Love cannot thrive where compulsion resides,

It blossoms in trust, where dignity abides.

When both choose to share in the act of love,

Kindness and warmth create a bond to rise above.

In harmony's dance, two souls intertwine,

Fulfilling their union, where both hearts align.

With compassion and care, they navigate the way,

Building a relationship that deepens each day.

So let love be cherished, as partners engage,

In the light of respect, they turn a new page.

For the essence of love lies in mutual embrace,

A journey of joy, marked by tenderness and grace.

Seek The Truth

While life flows through you, open ears can learn,

As truth whispers softly, your heart can discern.

In moments of clarity, knowledge takes flight,

But in the silence of death, there's no guiding light.

When disconnected from truth, the mind grows still,

A void where wisdom once sought to fulfill.

Awakening to the light, you must first strive,

To nurture the spark that keeps knowledge alive.

Embrace the journey, let your spirit awake,

For in seeking the truth, new pathways you'll make.

Life's essence unfolds when you choose to explore,

Each lesson a key to open new doors.

So honor this moment, let awareness arise,

In the dance of existence, find wisdom's prize.

For to be truly alive is to know and to see,

The beauty of truth, setting your spirit free.

WITH DIGNITY AND GRACE

You stand as few, amidst the throng,

Striving for truths where others feel wrong.

Materialism may cloud many a mind,

Yet your quest for what's real is both bold and refined.

Insults come forth from those who believe,

Labeling you opposers, unable to conceive,

That strength of character lies in your fight,

For understanding the world, for seeking the light.

In faith's fervor, they often forget,

The righteousness found in the paths you beget.

Your responsibility shines through the fray,

A conscientious pursuit that lights the way.

So carry your truths with dignity and grace,

For in the search for reality, we all have a place.

Let dialogue flourish, let respect be the guide,

In the quest for knowledge, let all voices reside.

BE CAUTIOUS

Be cautious with the words you share,

For open ears may soon disclose,

A trusted friend can lay you bare,

And turn your heart to whispered woes.

In moments fragile, tread with care,

For secrets linger, seeking light,

What's meant for one can find its air,

And shift your trust into the night.

A gentle listener may betray,

As words like shadows start to roam,

What once was safe can drift away,

And leave you feeling far from home.

So speak with wisdom, choose your muse,

For every ear can hold a tale,

In sharing burdens, you may lose,

The peace you sought, now turned to frail.

I Love You Truly

I love you truly, for we are all one,

Human beings connected, beneath the same sun;

In a shared destiny, our lives intertwine,

With thoughts and feelings that brightly align.

Let us love each other, let kindness arise,

In the mosaic of existence, let compassion be wise;

Every word and action can light up the way,

As we nurture the bonds that together we lay.

In this unfolding journey, let goodness be our guide,

In a world filled with struggles, let love be our pride;

For together we blossom, together we rise,

In the warmth of each other, true harmony lies.

So let us unite, with hearts open wide,

In this dance of life, let love be our guide;

For we are one essence, with strength in our care,

In the light of connection, we flourish and share.

THE CONNECTEDNESS

You've learned that all creatures share this ground,

Each life a collective, in harmony found.

The birds on their wings and fish in the sea,

Reflect the connectedness of you and me.

Every creature that runs, crawls, or takes flight,

Is part of a textile masterpiece woven together with light.

In their movements and calls, a language unfolds,

Whispering secrets that nature beholds.

From the smallest insect to the grandest beast,

Each plays a role, a vital feast.

In unity they thrive, a dance of the wild,

A reminder of kinship, pure and unspoiled.

So see in their journeys the truth of your own,

In every heartbeat, the spirit has grown.

For we are all bound in this web of life,

Together we flourish, amidst joy and strife.

THE LYRIANS AND VEGANS CAME

In ancient times, from distant stars,

The Lyrians and Vegans came,

Crossing realms, they journeyed far,

To Earth, where life ignited flame.

With Earthlings' kin, they forged a bond,

In passion's dance, and crafted hands,

Genetic art, a wondrous dawn,

New beings born to roam the lands.

From their union, giants rose,

Titans roamed with power and grace,

Creatures shaped by nature's prose,

In tales of old, they found their place.

But ages passed, and shadows grew,

Their kind declined, the world turned cold,

In time's held, they bid adieu,

As life evolved, their stories told.

TOGETHERNESS

What truly matters is how we embrace,

Each other's struggles, each heart's hidden space;

Though our burdens may feel heavy and deep,

Others bear shadows, where sorrow runs steep.

They wake in the morning, with hope fading low,

Searching for solace, for food, and for glow;

These times are demanding, yet still we can find,

The strength in Creation, a purpose aligned.

In the face of unkindness, let kindness prevail,

When rudeness encroaches, let respect be our sail;

Though pain may surround us, let compassion arise,

For ourselves and each other, let love be our prize.

Together we journey, through struggles we share,

In the vastness of being, let kindness declare;

For in every act of love, we discover our worth,

As we rise in the light, celebrating our birth.

In the absence of harmony

When family or society draws a line,

Creating divisions, where unity should shine,

No matter how noble the goals that they seek,

A fractured connection leaves progress weak.

In the absence of harmony, strength cannot thrive,

For together we flourish, together we strive.

True bonds of compassion must nurture and mend,

Only then can we rise, on each other depend.

If nations stand firm on "us" versus "them,"

The vision of togetherness wilts at the stem.

In isolation's grip, we drift far apart,

And kindness is stifled, eclipsing the heart.

Let's build a world where our spirits entwine,

Where love bridges gaps, and hope brightly shines.

In embracing our oneness, we'll finally see,

The strength of connection, our shared destiny.

NOT ALONE

In our vast Creation's cosmic span,

Diverse life forms emerge, each a plan.

Some from primates, familiar and near,

Others from reptiles, ancient and austere.

Amphibians flourish, bridging earth and sea,

Breathing in realms where poison runs free.

Gases lethal to us, sustaining their flight,

In alien domains where shadows ignite.

Close to suns blazing, they endure the heat,

Forging existence where our touch would retreat.

Far from stars' warmth, in icy domain,

They thrive in cold where few would remain.

Yet through this fabric of diverse design,

A singular intelligence intertwines.

From the dawn of creation to endless times,

Evolution's pulse beats in rhythmic chimes.

Learning, evolving, through epochs untold,

In the symphony of life, a story unfolds.

A unity in the grand cosmic plan,

Where all life weaves in the Absolut Absolutum's span.

In Every Thought And Feeling

To grasp the truth in creation's design,

It's not enough to follow the divine.

The laws of nature, virtues we acquire,

But deeper still lies a potent fire.

This energy flows from a spirit's core,

Animating life, urging us to explore.

With consciousness guiding our thoughts and our dreams,

It shapes our essence, or so it seems.

In each human heart, a creative force thrives,

Connecting our beings, where true life derives.

It's this spirit power that ignites our will,

A dynamic drive that calls us to fulfill.

So seek not just duty, but the energy within,

For through this creative spark, true growth can begin.

In every thought and feeling, let the spirit soar,

Embrace the depths of creation, and open every door.

Where Legacy Lie

The body's hardware, a fleeting design,

Crafts thoughts and feelings, through experience it shines,

Material consciousness learns and reflects,

A new life unfolds, with each soul it connects.

In the dance of existence, evolution takes flight,

A gathering of truths, in the depths of the night,

Knowledge compiles, a tapestry spun,

Layered in wisdom, forever begun.

This energy of creation, a radiant mass,

Built through the ages, as moments all pass,

Each insight preserved, like stars in the skies,

A reservoir of knowing, where legacy lies.

Though bodies may fade, and identities shift,

The essence of learning is a timeless gift,

In the heart of existence, our stories entwine,

An eternal progression, in wisdom divine.

LIFE AND DEATH

Life's continuum, eternal and vast,

In every form, existence steadfast.

Creation's energy within us all,

Animates, sustains, answers the call.

From human to beast, from plant to tree,

Connected in essence, bound and free.

Each part of nature, in harmony,

Shared in existence's symphony.

Death, not an end, but a cycle's flow,

Birth's companion, in life's grand show.

Two facets of the coin we hold,

In this journey, both are told.

THE SOURCE

In the stillness, energy breathes and swells,

A formless spark where creation dwells,

An essence that dances, both subtle and bold,

Awakening matter with stories untold.

Deep within each soul, a flicker resides,

A center of wisdom where knowledge abides,

Particles swirling in a timeless flight,

Carrying echoes of wisdom and light.

From the void emerges this vibrant decree,

The heart of existence, forever set free,

In each fleeting moment, it whispers and flows,

The source of our being, where true wonder grows.

Let us awaken to this sacred thread,

A tapestry woven where destinies spread,

In the pulse of creation, our spirits align,

Together we flourish, in unity's shine.

RACISM

In the fabric of our societal weave,

Lies the genesis of racism's seed,

Beyond individual hearts, it's found,

In beliefs entrenched, profound.

From ages past to present day,

These beliefs persist and sway,

Perpetuating bias deep within,

Fueling a cycle hard to thin.

An image upheld, a deity seen,

As white and supreme, it's been,

Embedded in collective thought,

Systemic structures tightly wrought.

Each acceptance, each nod,

Nurtures racism, deep and broad,

In our actions, in our creed,

Lies the root of its stubborn seed.

IN AQUARIAN GRACE

The human of the new age, in Aquarian grace,

Faces a challenge, a pivotal place.

With truth as their cornerstone, steady and strong,

They forge a foundation where all can belong.

In this era of insight, values expand,

Philosophies rooted in love's guiding hand.

Psychological wisdom begins to take flight,

Crafting a life filled with joy and with light.

Accepting freedom, they seek inner peace,

Unlocking potential, letting joy increase.

Each truth they uncover opens a door,

To a future where spirits can freely soar.

As they build this new vision, a world unfolds,

A fabric crafted with stories yet told.

In unity's warmth, they rise and ignite,

A new dawn of promise, radiant and bright.

IN PREVIOUS JOURNEYS

When one encounters the teachings that ignite,

It often reveals a past filled with light.

Stored impulses linger, guiding the way,

Echoes of lifetimes in the choices we play.

In previous journeys, wisdom takes form,

Leading the spirit through challenges warm.

If the call feels urgent, a fire in the night,

It's the path of awakening, drawing us right.

Yet when insights first touch the heart's door,

The process is gentle, unfolding with more.

Feelings arise like the dawn's early hue,

Awakening truths that feel fresh and new.

So honor the journey, however it flows,

Each moment a lesson, where understanding grows.

For in seeking the light, in the wisdom you find,

Awakens the spirit, expanding the mind.

THE SUBCONSCIOUS

Each new life, wisdom is shared

Within your essence, memories dwell,

Fragments of lifetimes, where stories compel.

The ego arises, a lens to reflect,

Awareness of self, in thoughts we collect.

Through cycles of rebirth, we learn and we grow,

In feelings and insights, our true selves we show.

Yet if shadows invade, the ego can stray,

Mistaking its nature, losing its way.

The subconscious safeguards wisdom profound,

Holding the lessons from lives all around.

In its quiet depths, knowledge awaits,

Guiding our journey, as each moment creates.

With each new life, this wisdom is shared,

A beacon of truth, though often impaired.

Seek clarity and love, let your spirit align,

For in understanding, your essence will shine.

THROUGH REBIRTH

Within your essence, memories dwell,

Fragments of lifetimes, where stories compel.

The ego arises, a lens to reflect,

Awareness of self, in thoughts we collect.

Through cycles of rebirth, we learn and we grow,

In feelings and insights, our true selves we show.

Yet if shadows invade, the ego can stray,

Mistaking its nature, losing its way.

The subconscious safeguards wisdom profound,

Holding the lessons from lives all around.

In its quiet depths, knowledge awaits,

Guiding our journey, as each moment creates.

With each new life, this wisdom is shared,

A beacon of truth, though often impaired.

Seek clarity and love, let your spirit align,

For in understanding, your essence will shine.

In Harmony's Song

Life is not a game, nor a fleeting hour,

But a journey deep, a call to power.

In duty's embrace and responsibility's hold,

We fulfill our purpose, as each story unfolds.

Through nurturing the self, our spirits ignite,

In the pursuit of wisdom, we seek the light.

Love and peace weave through each choice we make,

In harmony's song, a new dawn we awake.

Each step we take shapes the path ahead,

Crafting knowledge and joy in the words we've said.

As consciousness evolves, we rise and explore,

Creating a world rich with so much more.

Grasp this truth that guides our days,

Life's beauty lies in meaningful ways.

In love and freedom, together we stand,

Shaping a future, hand in hand.

ALIGNMENT

Though tiny as a needle's point, the spirit glows,

Its energy boundless, like a web it spreads wide,

Weaving through the body, where vibrant life flows,

Breathing into each cell, a luminous guide.

An intricate tapestry, fine threads intertwine,

It pulses with power, both gentle and vast,

Binding our essence, through spirit we shine,

Filling the heart with a joy that holds fast.

With every heartbeat, its presence flows free,

Invisible yet vital, a force that ignites,

Transforming the ordinary, revealing our key,

A dance of connection that nurtures our sights.

Though modest in size, its strength is profound,

It nourishes life in a rhythm divine,

A spirit that moves us, where love can be found,

Awakening our essence, eternally aligned.

THE TRUTH

In the depths where shadows linger, truth resides,

A steadfast force that cannot be denied.

Despite attempts to veil it in obscurity,

It rises, undeniable in its purity.

Even the most hesitant minds must concede,

As truth emerges from every hidden creed.

Efforts to cloak it in darkness fall in vain,

For truth prevails, relentless in its reign.

EARTH PEOPLE

People on Earth often take a stand,

Dictating lives with a heavy hand.

Their words like stones, they cast with might,

Yet sow discord, obscuring light.

In glassy homes, they dwell with pride,

While casting shadows they can't abide.

Hypocrisy hides behind the call,

For peace cannot thrive when barriers fall.

Every harsh word can fracture a soul,

In a world divided, we lose control.

To foster harmony, we must engage,

With empathy's warmth to turn the page.

Let's seek connection, let kindness flow,

In a life where love can grow.

For when we choose to lift and mend,

True peace emerges where hearts can blend.

THE RELIGIOUS SECTARIAN ENERGY

The phrase "The devil made me do it" reveals a hidden truth,

A notion tangled in shadows, diverging from convention.

Our world is ensnared by a rogue energy,

A dark force that sways even the seemingly wise.

This negativity influences many,

Like Billy Meier and others drawn to the strange,

Witnessing inexplicable moments while seeking the light.

I too have felt its subtle grip, steering thoughts awry.

Voices that urge unspeakable acts are not mere fantasies;

They resonate from a depth we cannot ignore.

Though we label them as demonic,

They often arise from those claiming divine belief.

In this struggle between light and dark,

The truth emerges, urging us to be vigilant.

For in the depths of despair lies the chance to misstep,

And within our hearts, the power to embrace the light.

FLAWLESS REALM

Each person must look within the glass,

To see themselves as they truly stand,

Not wrapped in dreams of a flawless realm,

But grounded in the truths at hand.

For none can dwell in perfect light,

Where every choice is clear and true,

We learn from stumbles and embrace our flaws,

In the shadows, growth comes into view.

Imperfections weave our common thread,

A rich tapestry of shared experience,

No one stands above another's path,

In this journey, we find our resilience.

So cherish the lessons that each misstep brings,

For wisdom flourishes in the heart's embrace,

In accepting ourselves, both flawed and whole,

We cultivate compassion in this human space.

THE DEEPER THE WOUNDS

In the realm of heartbreak, lessons bloom,

Amidst the ache, a chance to resume.

Though pain cuts deep, it's a crucible,

Where growth unfolds, undeniable.

Through shattered hopes and tear-stained nights,

We discover our strength, love's true heights.

Reflections cast on bonds once held,

Illuminate truths, stories unveiled.

In these poignant moments, we learn,

About desires, boundaries discern.

Self-awareness blossoms, clear and bright,

Guiding us towards relationships right.

Embrace heartbreak's transformative dance,

From its depths, new connections enhance.

For in the aftermath, we find our way,

To love more deeply, come what may.

HUMAN TAPESTRY

Within our human tapestry, let us see,

Equality's embrace, where hearts can be free.

Each person brings a story, a thread unique,

Weaving together in harmony we seek.

Valuing diversity, we humbly learn,

From every voice, new perspectives discern.

With humility and respect, bridges we mend,

Building trust, barriers transcend.

In this chorus of voices, rich and diverse,

Inclusivity blooms, a blessing to traverse.

Embracing differences, we grow and mend,

In unity's embrace, hearts blend.

RELENTLESS

In every heart lies the spark to grow,

Through struggle and effort, virtues flow.

A journey of learning, both deep and wide,

In shaping our character, we must abide.

With steadfast resolve, we forge our way,

In the quest for knowledge, day by day.

Let each lesson learned be a guiding light,

Illuminating paths through the darkest night.

Self-discipline calls, a lifelong embrace,

To seek understanding, to find our place.

In nurturing wisdom, our spirits align,

As we strive for greatness, one step at a time.

So never relent, let your quest be bold,

In the fabric of life, let your virtues unfold.

For in every moment, the chance to refine,

The essence of character, forever divine.

EACH DOOR

In each exchange, a chance unfolds,

To widen views, enrich our holds.

Attuned to human subtleties, we find,

Deep truths of life and hearts entwined.

Reflecting on each shared exchange,

Unveils insights, beyond the mundane.

Lessons hidden, waiting to be seen,

In conversations, spaces between.

Embracing every interaction's tale,

Curiosity fuels our quest to unveil.

No mere reaction, but a journey deep,

To learn, to grow, our hearts to keep.

This mindset guides with open eyes,

Seeking growth where insight lies.

Consciously engaging, we explore,

Life's lessons in each open door.

GUIDING LIGHT

In the silence of self-discovery's domain,

I forsake prayers, seeking inner terrain.

Confident strides, clarity's steady gaze,

Navigate my path through life's intricate maze.

With resolute heart without any belief,

I trust in my strength, dispelling all grief.

No need for external hands to guide,

My aspirations unfold from deep inside.

Each decision, a testament of my own,

In introspection's embrace, I've grown.

Determined steps, fueled by inner fire,

Manifesting dreams, higher and higher.

No reliance on fate or external plea,

But on self-assurance, steadfast and free.

Through challenges faced and lessons learned,

My journey unfolds, my spirit earned.

In this pursuit of purpose and zest,

I find fulfillment, in self-reliance blessed.

With introspection as my guiding light,

I forge my path, embracing each height.

THE BODY

The body serves as spirit's faithful guide,

A vessel of light where consciousness resides.

Not a prison, but a sacred home,

Where the radiant self is free to roam.

In this temple, life's essence glows,

The inner flame that endlessly flows.

It breathes creation, ignites the flame,

A luminous force that knows no name.

A castle strong, it holds great power,

Awakening dreams in each passing hour.

From stillness springs forth a vibrant dance,

Life unfolds in a boundless expanse.

Honor the body, a cherished embrace,

In its unity, we find our place.

Each heartbeat echoes the spirit's song,

A timeless journey where we all belong.

ART OF IGNORING

Mastering the art of ignoring,

A dance with distractions and priorities,

With focus sharpened, we can rise,

Embracing clarity, finding ease.

Selective attention, a guiding light,

Navigates challenges, steady and bright,

In the chaos of thoughts, we sift and choose,

Enhancing our well-being, we cannot lose.

When anger brews over words we see,

Why not just scroll, let it be?

Each mind is unique, like snowflakes fall,

Diverse in thought, we're one and all.

So guard your peace, it's yours to claim,

Nurture your spirit, let kindness reign,

In this journey of life, take heed and grow,

For your well-being, you owe it, this you know.

TURNING TO THE TRUTH

In the far future, a good life is ours,

If we turn to the truth that the spirit adores.

With teachings of life guiding our way,

A path of fulfillment awaits each new day.

Yet many have strayed, ignoring the signs,

Lost in the shadows where denial confines.

Turmoil and strife now cloud every heart,

As lovelessness lingers, tearing apart.

The prophets return, their forgiveness in hand,

Offering wisdom to help us withstand.

Though curses were spoken and truth cast aside,

They come back anew, with love as their guide.

Embrace their teachings, let harmony grow,

For in unity's light, the spirit will glow.

A chance for redemption, a fresh start in sight,

With truth as your beacon, walk boldly in light.

MATERIALISM

In the celestial expanse, stars gleam bright,
Devoid of life, yet casting celestial light.
A metaphor for desires that burn deep,
In pursuit of shine, materialism's keep.
Connection to essence, a cosmic thread,
Creation's energy, in each being spread.
Integral to the Universal whole,
Evolution's path, wisdom as its goal.
Amidst glittering allure, hold true,
To life's genuine illumination, pursue.
Let not material distractions sway,
From the essence of being, day by day.

YOURSELF IN OTHERS

In the mirror of another's gaze,

A chance to learn and to appraise,

If flaws are seen, and faults appear,

Look inward first, without a fear.

For change begins where insight gleams,

Not by judgment, but in dreams,

Of better selves we wish to find,

Through empathy and grace combined.

So let us heed this timeless call,

To grow and rise, and stand tall,

For what we shift within our core,

Will ripple out and heal much more.

THE CLEAR PATH

Belief mixed with untruth breeds fear and doubt,

Anxieties grow where shadows call out.

Turn to the truth, let its light break the chain,

For in knowing, you'll find freedom from pain.

In truth's gentle glow, find solace and peace,

As the fear of death fades, anxieties cease.

Embrace the clear path, let wisdom arise,

Transforming your spirit, revealing the skies.

Seek understanding, let your heart lead the way,

For knowledge brings courage, brightening each day.

Step into the light, release what confines,

In the realm of truth, your spirit aligns.

Let go of the doubts that cloud your own view,

Walk boldly toward truth, let its strength renew.

In this quest for clarity, you'll rise and stand tall,

Free from the shadows, empowered through all.

JESUS CHRIST

In the echoes of history's grasp,

Jesus Christ, a name ensnared,

Binding minds in chains of the past,

As long as this guise is revered.

666, the mark of the unseen,

The anti-logo in shadows cast,

Keeps consciousness in a bind,

Until truth's light breaks free at last.

Let minds awaken to the call,

Beyond illusions, beyond the fray,

To forge a path where freedom thrives,

And rewrite the tale of yesterday.

IGNORANCE

In the shadows where doubts reside,

Lies a call to shed ignorance's pride.

Cease the refrain of "I know naught,"

Embrace instead the seeker's thought.

Cast off the cloak of unyielding belief,

Embrace the journey to seek relief.

For belief alone cannot quench the thirst,

To unravel mysteries, to understand first.

Let curiosity be your guiding light,

In pursuit of truths, shining bright.

Embrace the path where knowledge grows,

From uncertainty to what wisdom bestows.

Mohamed

In the desert's embrace, where stars ignite,

Mohamed was born, a beacon of light.

February's embrace, five seventy-one,

A prophet destined, as day meets the sun.

Against a tide of bloodshed and fear,

He spoke of peace, his message clear.

To quell the storm of a cult's wild spree,

And save humanity, his destiny.

Yet echoes of his words did fade,

Twisted and turned, as memories swayed.

Like Jmmanuel's tale, altered in time,

His teachings shifted, a subtle chime.

Prophet Mohamed, in history's scroll,

A guide and leader, of heart and soul.

From Mecca's sands to eternity's frame,

His legacy endures, aflame.

COMPASSION

Do not strike at those who stumble and fall,

Nor punish the thieves, the deceivers, the small.

For vengeance breeds pain and darkness in kind,

Seek fairness and mercy, with justice aligned.

Manslayers should not face death for their wrong,

But find atonement where healing is strong.

The primal laws guide us toward grace,

Emphasizing compassion in every space.

Practice forbearance, forgiveness, and peace,

For reconciliation is where true healing can cease.

Let every response be rooted in care,

In a world of humanity, kindness we share.

Teach the fallible to heed the signs,

To reflect on their actions, to mend broken lines.

With understanding and love, let transformation start,

Building a future where healing is art.

Our Time

In this time, truth eludes most

Earth-bound souls,

Engrossed in living, their pursuit unfolds.

To them, life's essence is all that's clear,

No room for truths they cannot see or hear.

On their last breath, reflections pierce the air,

Questions arise of paths laid bare.

Yet amidst this existential strife,

Billy Meier's teachings stir new life.

Creation's wisdom beckons from afar,

A promise of change, a rising star.

So close, yet distant, humanity's plight,

Truth's tidal wave prepares to ignite.

Billy Meier, herald of cosmic grace,

In nature's cycle, truth finds its place.

As waves of revelation start to swell,

Truth's surge begins, with tales to tell.

BELIEVE

Cease this word's sharp edge, its piercing sting,

Let silence reign, where peace can bring.

For in Nothingness, beliefs find rest,

Especially in oneself, where truth is blessed.

Know thyself, in depths profound,

Where inner voices softly sound.

No need for outward boasts or cries,

In quiet knowing, strength shall rise.

In Nothing's embrace, serenity found,

Amidst the chaos, a steady ground.

Self-understanding, a radiant flame,

In stillness, where whispers proclaim.

Uncovering Lies

The light of truth is often veiled,

By those who harm, their conscience curtailed.

In shadows they speak, twisting the word,

Seeking profit while justice is blurred.

With masks of deceit, they mask their intent,

As they profit from pain, their morals bent.

But truth, like a flame, will not be contained,

Its purity shines through all that's profaned.

In the depths of darkness, let us be the light,

Uncovering lies, making wrongs into right.

For in the face of greed, we must stand tall,

And honor the truth, embracing the call.

So let us unveil what's hidden from sight,

Championing justice, igniting the right.

For together we rise, and together we see,

The power of truth setting humanity free.

THE MOON

When asked of the moon and the stars' role,

Share how the moon shapes the tides and the whole.

It influences waters, drawing them near,

Creating the rhythms that life holds dear.

Its pull affects weather, in cycles so vast,

Nurturing growth, from the present to past.

Through phases it guides, both gentle and strong,

Inspiring all life to flourish and throng.

The stars, too, twinkle with wisdom and lore,

Mapping the heavens, inviting us to explore.

Together they shine, a celestial dance,

Reminding us all of our cosmic romance.

So speak of the moon and the stars in the night,

Of their purpose in nature, their beauty and light.

For in their vast movements, a harmony shows,

Connecting our lives to the universe's flows.

True Freedom

A human being must never wear a yoke,

Nor yield to the weight of another's cloak.

In freedom, we rise, embracing our place,

Fulfilling our duties with dignity and grace.

No soul should be bound by authority's might,

For true strength is found in standing for what's right.

With resolve, we act, regardless of scorn,

Choosing our path, though others may mourn.

In the face of rebuke, let courage prevail,

For freedom's sweet promise will never grow stale.

We honor our duty, even when challenged,

With the heart of a warrior, unbowed and unblemished.

So walk with conviction, uphold what is true,

In a world that may question, let your spirit break through.

For within each of us lies a power profound,

To shape a future where freedom is found.

SPIRIT

In realms where spirit reigns, untouched by time,
Unblemished essence, sublime and prime.
No wrong can stain its luminous domain,
Where purity and light forever reign.
Yet in the dance of life, 'tis consciousness that thrives,
Navigating earthly realms, where soul survives.
It's not the spirit's form that walks the earth,
But consciousness that experiences birth.
Material world, a fleeting masquerade,
Through which the spirit's essence softly fades.
In unseen realms, where truth's eternal flame,
Consciousness and spirit intertwine, the same.

Embracing Transparency

Request always for truth and clarity to reign,

For in honest dialogue, we break every chain.

Each soul connected to what's genuine and bright,

Cultivates a world where love ignites.

When truth is shared, misunderstandings cease,

Fostering connections that nurture peace.

With clarity guiding us, we pave the way,

Towards a future where compassion holds sway.

For only through honesty can we truly rise,

In a world well-led, where hope never dies.

Embracing transparency, let our voices unite,

Transforming our lives in the warmth of the light.

Together we journey, on this shared quest,

Creating a reality where clarity is blessed.

In wisdom and kindness, may we play our part,

Building a tomorrow that springs from the heart.

The Cosmic Law

In the vast expanse of cosmic mind,

No room for vengeance can you find.

Lessons woven into life's design,

Through actions taught, through paths we wind.

Cause and effect, the cosmic law,

Shapes our journey, what we saw.

We mold our reality, day by day,

Creating futures along the way.

To alter the world, each human must seek,

Within themselves, where change runs deep.

Transformation blooms from within,

A new era dawns, where love shall begin.

DEEP

Deep within us lies a truth profound,

A whisper of something beyond the ground,

A source of our thoughts and feelings refined,

A spirit that stirs in the depths of the mind.

This insight reveals we are more than we see,

Not bound by the material, we yearn to be free,

For the life we perceive is but one fleeting stage,

A deeper existence, a wisdom, a sage.

Throughout the ages, this truth has been sought,

Philosophers ponder, and seekers have thought,

That within each of us shines an eternal light,

A spirit undying, forever in flight.

Though the world may distract, and efforts may tire,

This inner reality fuels our desire,

For in knowing ourselves, we awaken our core,

To the infinite essence we endlessly explore.

CLARITY

Always seek to clarify the path ahead,

For understanding blossoms where clear words are said.

In the light of questions, discord fades away,

Replacing strife and hatred with peace's gentle sway.

Let not confusion mar the bonds we share,

In seeking truth, approach with utmost care.

For when we listen, hearts begin to blend,

Creating harmony, where kindness can mend.

In every dialogue, let patience be the guide,

Fostering connections where love can abide.

For rightness in behavior is found in the trust,

That mutual respect will turn conflict to dust.

So speak with intention, and hear with an open heart,

From this foundation, let understanding start.

In clarity and compassion, we find our way,

Building a world where peace holds sway.

GREED

Do not consume your wealth with lies and deceit,

Nor let greed and stinginess shape your seat.

Refrain from bribery, let fairness prevail,

For to seek gain through wrong is to set your own trail.

In dealings with others, let honesty guide,

Avoid the temptation to let greed coincide.

For every act of unright takes its toll,

Devouring the trust that connects every soul.

Live in equitableness, uphold what is true,

For integrity nurtures a bond that is due.

In striving for wealth, let virtue be your aim,

For through honest endeavor, you build not just fame.

So cherish your riches, let kindness increase,

In the wealth of the spirit, find true lasting peace.

For the path of integrity shines brighter each day,

Leading all toward a brighter, more just way.

NOAHKADNOSSER

In ages past, a builder stood,
Noahkadnosser, man of peace,
With wisdom vast, he heard the call,
From Zebalon, the cosmic breeze.
A comet's wrath approached the land,
A warning shared from worlds afar,
Together, they forged an Ark so grand,
To shelter life beneath the stars.
Through flood's fierce tide, the family sailed,
With beasts of earth in unity,
Their story whispered, time unveiled,
Transformed through ages, lost in memory.
Now Noah's name, a tale refined,
In sacred texts, the truth concealed,
Yet echoes of the cosmic mind,
In legends vast, remain revealed.

IDEAS

In the symphony of voices, each a spark,

Gratitude blooms for the paths they mark,

For every view, whether near or far,

Expands the horizons where truths spar.

In the mosaic of ideas, vivid and grand,

Differences weave, hand in hand,

Each perspective a brushstroke bold,

Painting wisdom, a tale retold.

For in the harmony of dissent and accord,

Growth emerges, from discourse stirred,

Thankful hearts, in unity stirred.

STAND TALL

Each person must shape their own path clear,

Embracing justice, honesty, and reason's light,

In every action, let virtue unfold,

As thoughts and feelings guide the flight.

In consciousness and character, we grow,

Nurturing the psyche through intention's care,

With every choice, let integrity bloom,

Creating a life that's bold and rare.

Forge that inner spark to rise anew,

Stand tall against the weight of doubt,

For true humility is strength combined,

A self-empowerment that speaks out.

In this journey of crafting who you are,

Let the spirit flourish, vibrant and free,

For in authentic living, life finds grace,

And every step reveals your true decree.

IN THE ECHOES OF SILENCE

In the echoes of silence, where shadows creep,

The truth emerges from secrets deep,

Unshackled from chains of fear and guile,

It speaks with a force that defies denial.

No glamour or guise can sway its course,

For the truth is a river, steady and force,

It carves through deception with uncompromising grace,

Leaving falsehoods shattered in its steadfast embrace.

In the tapestry of life, where lies may abound,

The truth stands firm, unswayed and unbound,

In its unwavering gaze, clarity unfurls,

The truth gives no fuck to the webs of the world.

TESLA

In Tesla's heart, a secret burned,

A brilliance to the world unturned,

Inventions spun from dreams profound,

Yet hidden, safe from chaos' sound.

For Tesla knew the danger dire,

If his creations fueled the fire,

Of wars that ravage land and soul,

His genius bound to a higher goal.

In silence, he crafted wonders rare,

A shield against the world's despair,

A mind that sparked with innovation,

Guarded by silent dedication.

So in the quiet of his design,

Tesla's light would ever shine,

A beacon of hope in troubled days,

His secret kept in silent ways.

THE CREATOR OVERLORDS

In Lyra's distant celestial expanse,

The Creator Overlords faltered in their genetic dance.

Unable to wield their own power's might,

They birthed a race destined to fight.

Humans scattered across Earth's domain,

Carrying traits of cruelty and pain.

Limited by life's fleeting span,

Bound by design since time began.

Seeking solace in Sol's gentle glow,

Amidst the stars where secrets flow.

Yet shackled by their maker's hand,

A fate embedded in their genetic strand.

To break free, to transcend the past,

We must rewrite our genetic cast.

Unravel the chains that bind our souls,

Embrace a destiny where freedom rolls.

ALTRUISTIC LOVE

Altruistic love, a luminous thread,

Binding us all, where compassion is spread.

It reflects the unity of life's grand design,

In the vastness of the cosmos, our spirits align.

This love flows like rivers, endless and free,

Connecting each heart, from sea to sea.

In the twinkling of stars and the rustling leaves,

It whispers of harmony, the peace that it weaves.

An expression of kindness, a gift we all share,

In the light of our actions, we nurture and care.

Through simple gestures, the universe glows,

In the warmth of our hearts, true love overflows.

So let us embody this infinite grace,

In every connection, find our rightful place.

Altruistic hearts, together we stand,

In the embrace of existence, hand in hand.

ASTRONAUT

Upon Earth, no astronauts tread, only pilots in flight,

In realms where Earth's grasp gently yields,

True space emerges, where destiny wields its might.

To the moon's edge pilots journey, bound and free,

Earth's gravity lingers, a steadfast company.

Yet beyond the moon's tranquil domain,

Lies the realm where cosmic mysteries reign,

Where sun and galaxy intertwine in cosmic dance,

Astronauts explore, in celestial trance.

In this cosmic arena, where gravity's hold bends,

They navigate realms where wonder transcends,

Beyond earthly confines, in infinite grace,

Discovering the universe, an eternal embrace.

No Commandments

The primal wellspring, creation's core,

Offers laws of life, not commands to ignore,

Unlike the divinities shaped by hands,

Crafted illusions that mislead and strand.

For those who mock the truths that bind,

Lead seekers astray, leaving wisdom behind,

Chasing false shadows, they seek to escape,

From ignorance cloaked in a comforting shape.

Yet in the heart of genuine light,

Lies the path to understanding, pure and bright,

Embracing the laws that nature provides,

Unveiling the truth where true knowledge abides.

So seek not refuge in fantasies spun,

But in the essence of all that is one,

For only through wisdom can we rise above,

Finding our place in the embrace of love.

Exists A Spice

Exists a spice, revered and bright,

A treasure of healing, a beacon of light,

In its presence, ailments retreat and hide,

Cancer and viruses cannot abide.

Black cumin, a name whispered through time,

Not sesame's kin, but a remedy sublime,

With powers to conquer inflammation's strife,

A guardian of health, restoring life.

From ulcers to diabetes, it boldly defends,

A panacea known, where healing transcends,

Historic in wisdom, a remedy profound,

In nature's embrace, true solace is found.

Yet death remains sovereign, untouched by this grace,

But hope lingers on in this sacred space,

For within this small seed lies potential so vast,

A testament to healing, a future steadfast.

THE MOTHERS OF THE MILLENNIUM

In distant days, the balance will change,

As woman rises, the world rearranged,

No longer will man alone hold the crown,

For she'll steer the fate of a new, shared town.

As mother of Earth, her voice will be strong,

Dismantling tyranny, righting the wrong,

With wisdom as her scepter, she'll guide the way,

Ending the age of war's harsh display.

The echoes of violence will fade into night,

As she nurtures peace, igniting the light,

No more will the past's brutal shadow loom,

In her embrace, a new dawn will bloom.

In this time of healing, hope will emerge,

With compassion and strength, she'll lead the surge,

Together we'll build a world reborn,

Where love and unity are proudly worn.

THE BIBLE

In ancient scrolls where tales were spun,

Truths and myths together run,

Twelve prophets, their minds ablaze,

In forty days, a sacred maze.

First Torah lost in fiery plight,

Second born from prophets' light,

From oral lore and ancient rhymes,

Myths and truths through timeless times.

Not a chronicle of history's breath,

Nor a testament to life or death,

Christianity's cloak, borrowed and spun,

From Jewish myths, its journey begun.

Jmmanuel, beyond their creed,

Taught of Creation's eternal seed,

From Enoch's line, wisdom pure,

Beyond mere tales, spirit secure.

REINCARNATION

In cycles unseen, we are born anew,
Bound by laws of reincarnation true.
From earthly forms, our spirits ascend,
To realms where journeys find their blend.
In Beyond's embrace, where spirits roam,
Learning truths that call us home.
Through deaths and lives, we strive to find,
Unity with Creation's cosmic mind.
Evolution's path, spirit and soul entwine,
In each life lived, a chance to refine.
Through endless cycles, we seek to be,
One with Creation's harmony.
Thus, in the dance of eternity's flow,
We evolve, spirit and consciousness grow.
Through reincarnation's sacred art,
We journey toward the cosmic heart.

HELL

In the depths where burns cut deep and severe,

Where flesh and bone succumb, yet oddly veer,

Nerve endings singed, pain's grip undone,

A paradox unfolds 'neath the blazing sun.

Third-degree scars, where agony should reign,

Yet strangely, in this infernal domain,

Silent echoes trace the wounds that swell,

No anguish stirs where torment should dwell.

Thus, my point stands firm, bold and clear,

In realms imagined, or perhaps sincere,

No hell can claim where pain's denied,

For where pain's absent, peace may reside.

WHEN DREAMS RESONATE

In the heart's bold dance, dreams take flight,

Nothing is hard if it's a goal in sight.

With steadfast gaze, the horizon calls,

Where challenges fade, and courage enthralls.

Through trials deep and mountains high,

Every hurdle met, we dare to defy.

Each step a testament, a journey's grace,

In the soul's embrace, fears we erase.

For in the crucible of will and desire,

Stars align, ambitions never tire.

With passion's fire, we shape our fate,

Nothing is hard when dreams resonate.

Follow The Signs

You cannot claim that signs were never shared,

For prophets spoke the truth, their wisdom bared.

Time and again, the teachings have been clear,

Yet in your heart, you turned away from fear.

The lessons of spirit and life's guiding light,

Have come to you often, shining through the night.

But with contempt, you chose to look away,

Now burdened by the void, you seek to sway.

Each moment missed, a chance to understand,

Now calls you back to grasp the guiding hand.

The truth is waiting, though you've wandered far,

It flickers softly like a distant star.

So take the time to seek what's always near,

Embrace the lessons whispered in your ear.

For in the search, you'll find a path anew,

A journey toward the wisdom meant for you.

OVERPOPULATION

Once a formula, now lost to the night,
Guided souls in the afterlife's flight,
Age of death by one point five-two,
Now fades, as cycles quicken anew.
Creation's energies hasten the birth,
Souls reincarnate, misplaced on Earth,
Memories stir, past lives unwind,
Incomplete reprogramming, undefined.
Creation shares no blame, but us alone,
Humanity's rush, seeds they have sown,
"Go forth and multiply," they repeat,
Ignoring warnings, our planet deplete.
We plead with hearts open wide,
Mitigate overpopulation's stride,
For Billy's wisdom must guide,
Echoes of truth we cannot hide.

AUTONOMY

On Earth, voices echo far and wide,

Eager to shape how others abide.

But autonomy's essence they hold dear,

Rejecting commands that draw near.

In life's intricate weave, paths unfold,

Each story unique, a tale to be told.

Freedom cherished, in every soul's quest,

Resisting constraints, they manifest.

Let understanding guide our way,

In honoring choices, let empathy sway.

For Earth's myriad lives to thrive and ignite,

Autonomy cherished, in freedom's light.

Be Like Water

Be like water, in its essence pure,
Flowing through realms, forever endure.
From mountain springs to ocean vast,
Shape-shifting form, embracing contrast.
No obstacle halts its steady course,
Adapting, yielding without remorse.
Through cracks and crevices, it finds its way,
In endless motion, night and day.
Reflecting sunlight, calming storm,
A mirror to life, in its truest form.
Be like water, in every flow,
In stillness deep, in rapid go.
With patience and grace, it softly bends,
Around each barrier, it amends.
Be like water, serene and clear,
Navigating life, without fear.

From Within

From the depths within, all springs forth,

Life's tapestry woven, threads of thought,

Every breath a whisper, every beat a tale,

In the heart's chamber, where dreams set sail.

Peace, elusive yet ever sought,

In the labyrinth of being, where battles fought,

Victory not in conquest, but in serene embrace,

Where storms relent, and calm finds its place.

Within, the universe unfolds,

Secrets whispered, stories untold,

Inner peace, the soul's sacred song,

Where echoes of eternity belong.

The ultimate triumph, quiet and deep,

Not in worldly acclaim, nor treasures keep,

But in the stillness, where truth resides,

Where the spirit abides, serene and wise.

GETTING EVEN

In the quiet of the dusk's gentle glow,

Lies the secret that few truly know,

To embrace peace, let bitterness go,

Refrain from getting even, let compassion flow.

For in the storm of anger's roar,

Lies a calm that seeks to restore,

Hearts that ache, bruised and sore,

Through forgiveness, healing we implore.

Let the echoes of discord cease,

In the embrace of gentle release,

Where kindness reigns and troubles decrease,

Refrain from getting even, find inner peace.

NURTURING

Do not waste your idealism bright,

On fleeting things that lack true worth,

Instead, direct it toward your core,

To unearth the self that gives you birth.

In striving to improve and grow,

You touch the essence deep within,

Connecting with the drive for change,

Where progress and success begin.

This true self forms the solid ground,

A base for living life with aim,

Guiding you through each choice and trial,

Illuminating paths that bear your name.

So nurture this spirit, let it shine,

For in its light, fulfillment calls,

With every step toward your true being,

You build a life where purpose enthralls.

THE WISE SPEAKS LESS

In silence, wisdom finds its abode,

Where words, once rampant, now take pause.

For in the quiet spaces, truths unfold,

A symphony of stillness, without applause.

The wiser one becomes, the less they say,

Their thoughts a canvas in shades of gray.

Each syllable chosen with utmost care,

To convey depths only silence can dare.

In whispers of insight, the world takes heed,

In silence, the soul finds what it needs.

For speech may fill the air with sound,

But wisdom thrives where silence is found.

INNER PEACE

Amidst the cacophony of daily strife,

Where voices clamor for attention's life,

A steady heart knows when to stay composed,

And let the barking dogs remain unopposed.

In the symphony of chaos and despair,

Where echoes clash in the relentless air,

A peaceful soul discerns the quiet path,

Ignoring discord with a gentle laugh.

For every bark that seeks to stir the storm,

There lies a wisdom in remaining warm,

To choose the peace that soothes the troubled mind,

And leave the clamor of the world behind.

PLANET OVER COUNTRY

In this vast universe, where galaxies swirl and dance,
I declare my allegiance to Earth's expansive expanse.
Above man-made borders and flags unfurled,
I choose the planet, the home of all, our shared world.
Give me oceans that stretch to the horizon's rim,
Where waves crash and creatures dive deep within.
Mountains soaring high, touching clouds above,
Whisper tales of ages, of endurance and love.
In the cradle of forests, where tranquility reigns,
Amongst towering trees and creatures with no chains,
Here, I find my refuge, my heart's true chime,
I'll take planet over country every single time.

Soul's Sacred Song

From the depths within, all springs forth,

Life's fabric woven, threads of thought,

Every breath a whisper, every beat a tale,

In the heart's chamber, where dreams set sail.

Peace, elusive yet ever sought,

In the labyrinth of being, where battles fought,

Victory not in conquest, but in serene embrace,

Where storms relent, and calm finds its place.

Within, the universe unfolds,

Secrets whispered, stories untold,

Inner peace, the soul's sacred song,

Where echoes of eternity belong.

The ultimate triumph, quiet and deep,

Not in worldly acclaim, nor treasures keep,

But in the stillness, where truth resides,

Where the spirit abides, serene and wise.

IGNORING

Amidst the cacophony of daily strife,

Where voices clamor for attention's life,

A steady heart knows when to stay composed,

And let the barking dogs remain unopposed.

In the symphony of chaos and despair,

Where echoes clash in the relentless air,

A peaceful soul discerns the quiet path,

Ignoring discord with a gentle laugh.

For every bark that seeks to stir the storm,

There lies a wisdom in remaining warm,

To choose the peace that soothes the troubled mind,

And leave the clamor of the world behind.

SELF PLEASURE

Both woman and man have the right to explore,

To find pleasure within, to seek and restore.

Self-gratification, a natural embrace,

In harmony with creation, it finds its place.

It's woven in nature, a part of the design,

To honor the self, and in pleasure, to shine.

No laws are broken when joy is pursued,

For in understanding our bodies, we're renewed.

This exploration fosters a deeper connection,

With self and with others, in love's reflection.

In the joy of the moment, let freedom arise,

Celebrating desire, where authenticity lies.

So embrace your own pleasure, with grace and with ease,

For it's part of our being, a gift to release.

In the dance of existence, let joy take its stand,

For both woman and man, in unity hand in hand...

pun intended!

UNITY

In a world where every soul walks its path alone,

Self-interest prevailing, hearts turned to stone.

But envision a world where bonds are deep and strong,

Where unity and care right all that's wrong.

Picture a dawn where compassion reigns supreme,

Where selflessness replaces the selfish scheme.

In the fabric of existence, threads tightly weave,

A tapestry of kindness, where all can live.

Beyond the realm of survival's lonely call,

A universe where empathy conquers all.

To live not just for oneself, but for each other's sake,

Where love and understanding forever awake.

Imagine a future where hands reach across divide,

Where humanity's spirit soars high and wide.

For every gesture of love, big or small,

Echoes through eternity, embracing one and all.

LONG AGO

Long ago, humanity set its thought aside,

Independent minds lost, with time as their guide,

Now shackled by powers that govern and sway,

In a web of deceit, they've wandered astray.

Ensnared by the lies of those who mislead,

Struggling to grasp the truth they so need,

Faith turned to blindness, they follow the throng,

Oblivious to chains that keep them from strong.

In their trust, they are used, their hearts filled with strife,

Manipulated hopes lead to shadows of life,

Fueled by revenge, they succumb to the night,

Turning against peace, embracing the fight.

Yet within every heart lies a spark yet untamed,

A chance to awaken, to rise unashamed,

Reclaiming their thoughts, they can break every chain,

Transforming their sorrow into wisdom's gain.

O Souls

Most of humanity lives in chains unseen,
Bound by the doctrines of what might have been,
Afraid to embrace the weight of their choice,
They follow the falsehoods, silencing their voice.
Governments and creeds weave tales that deceive,
While seekers of truth quietly grieve,
In their quiet surrender, their spirits grow dim,
Forsaking the quest for the light that's within.
As initiative wanes, they drift with the tide,
Ignoring the spark of knowledge inside,
Yet deep in their hearts, a yearning remains,
For clarity, wisdom, and breaking the chains.
Awaken, O souls, to the strength you possess,
To question the shadows, to strive for progress,
For in seeking the truth, you'll uncover the way,
To rise from the darkness and embrace the day.

THE SPHERE OF THE DEAD

When the body fades, the spirit takes flight,

Entering a realm beyond our sight,

A sphere of the dead, where shadows play,

The comprehensive consciousness finds its way.

Here, the essence processes all left undone,

Experiences gathered, the struggles begun,

In this timeless expanse, the soul reflects,

On lessons unlearned and paths to connect.

As time flows softly, the work comes to close,

Unraveling mysteries, as wisdom bestows,

Transcending the burdens of the past's heavy weight,

The spirit transforms, embracing its fate.

In neutrality's cradle, the self gently wanes,

The personality slips, releasing its chains,

And in this release, a new journey takes flight,

As the cycle of life dances into the light.

THE INFINITE'S GRACE

Within each heart lies a sacred spark,

A glimpse of Creation, igniting the dark.

In our essence, we carry a shared thread,

A journey toward oneness where all paths are led.

Every being reflects the infinite's grace,

A dance of connection in time and space.

In seeking the depths, we find our way,

United in purpose, come what may.

Our innermost nature whispers of peace,

An invitation to love, where doubts cease.

In this boundless expanse, we learn and grow,

Embracing the truth that we all come to know.

Together we rise, hearts intertwined,

In the symphony of life, we are designed.

For in the arms of Creation's light,

We find our belonging, our shared birthright.

WHEN DEATH ARRIVES

Even when death arrives, a soft final breath,

The spirit within us knows naught of death,

A seer, a witness, forever alive,

A spark of Creation, where energies thrive.

For within us resides a timeless essence,

A piece of the cosmos, pure in its presence,

Eternal and vast, it flows through the night,

In the heart of consciousness, a boundless light.

Though bodies may wither and fade with the years,

The spirit endures, beyond all our fears,

A whisper of life that cannot be tamed,

In the cycle of being, forever unclaimed.

So when shadows gather and the end seems near,

Know the light within you will always be here,

Part of the whole, your journey unfolds,

An eternal connection that Creation holds.

GOD

In shadows deep, your heart bears weight,

Sadness cloaked in thoughts that isolate.

When truth is spoken by the prophets wise,

You turn in rage, dismissing their clear skies.

Accusing them of falsehood, you deny,

The signs they offer, marvels passing by.

You label their gifts as tricks of the night,

Rejecting the light for shadows out of sight.

In anger, you defend your crafted gods,

Tin figures that crumble beneath heavy odds.

Yet in your heart, a flicker still remains,

A whisper of truth that calls through the chains.

Embrace the light that seeks to guide your way,

For in the truth, your spirit may sway.

Release the rage, let wisdom take its place,

And find your peace within love's warm embrace.

Bold & Logical

The humans of Earth, in shadows, have strayed,

Forgetting the power of thought they once displayed,

Lost in the echoes of voices that bind,

Neglecting the logic that sharpens the mind.

In a world filled with noise, the truth often fades,

Rational choices obscured by the charades,

They follow the currents, swept along by the tide,

While wisdom and reason quietly reside.

Yet within every heart lies a spark still aglow,

A reminder of thinking, of choices to grow,

To reclaim the essence of logic and light,

And navigate darkness, emerging in sight.

Let us awaken, embrace what we hold,

To question, to ponder, to be brave and bold,

For the strength of our minds can guide us anew,

In the dance of existence, where clarity shines through.

Consciousness

When spirit-energy enters a human frame,
The creative law awakens, igniting the flame,
A counterpart needed, the balance is sought,
Creating a consciousness where matter is caught.
This union of forces, a dance of the poles,
The positive spirit energizes the souls,
As the cycle of life begins to unfold,
Through countless reincarnations, wisdom is gold.
From this moment of birth, a new spirit takes flight,
Evolving through matter, through darkness and light,
Gathering power, both earthly and divine,
In realms of awareness where mysteries align.
For four hundred twenty billion years it will grow,
A journey through existence, where insights bestow,
Until merging with Creation, a universal thread,
Becoming one with all, where consciousness is led.

OMEDAM

A human spirit seeks a form to call home,

Only in OMEDAM does it freely roam,

When a spacetraveler's journey comes to an end,

The spirit ventures forth, on new paths to transcend.

In search of a world where new life can thrive,

It enters a vessel, keeping the spark alive,

Though separate from roots of its former race,

Shared evolution binds them in time and space.

Human spiritforms find their place in the flesh,

Exclusively in humans, where traits intertwine fresh,

Not in insects or animals, nor plants of the earth,

For their essence is tied to humanity's birth.

Each new incarnation offers chances anew,

A dance through existence, where all life is true,

As the spirit journeys through realms yet unknown,

Finding purpose and meaning, forever its own.

THREE BRIEF HOURS

The spirit-energy lingers, a fleeting glow,

For three brief hours, before it must go,

When the spirit departs, leaving shadows behind,

Yet remnants remain, in the body confined.

This residual essence, a trace of the soul,

Holds the potential for life to make whole,

In the hands of nature, it softly blends,

As warmth fades away, the cycle transcends.

Absorbed by the earth, by the air, by the sea,

A whisper of life in a silent decree,

What once was a vessel, now part of the ground,

In the dance of existence, all life is unbound.

Thus, even in loss, there's a beauty we find,

In the spirit's departure, a gift left behind,

A chance for renewal, for life to extend,

As nature reclaims what the heart cannot end.

THE SPIRIT

The spirit, an idea, vibrant and pure,
An essence of energy, destined to endure,
Born from creation, in cosmic design,
Evolving through ages, transcending the divine.
Indestructible force, eternally bright,
A loving presence, guiding through night,
In the mind's quiet chamber, it finds its place,
Growing and shifting with infinite grace.
In the superior colliculus, thoughts take flight,
Where perception awakens, revealing the light,
A spark of awareness in the brain's vast expanse,
Navigating existence, a mystical dance.
In the frontal cortex, our essence expands,
Crafting our stories, as life's journey commands,
Forever transforming, in wisdom's embrace,
The spirit within us, a boundless space.

THE BOND

In freedom's light, we boldly tread,

With choices unbound, where passions are fed.

As long as our steps bring no sorrow or strife,

We unveil the purpose, the essence of life.

Awakening stirs in the depths of our soul,

The true ego rises, becoming the whole.

In moments of silence, our truths come to sight,

Guiding our journey through shadows and light.

With dreams in our hearts, we navigate fate,

Creating our stories, embracing our state.

Though we stumble and soar, in unity we stand,

Each thread in the fabric, a shared, gentle hand.

Let us cherish this wisdom, as we roam free,

In kindness and love, we discover what's key.

For life's sweetest meaning unfolds as we see,

In the bonds that unite us, we find harmony.

Teachers And Prophets

When the moment dawns for life's rebirth,

Higher spirits emerge as guiding light,

Teachers and prophets, revealing their worth,

Leading the way through shadows of night.

Bound by laws of creation, they inspire,

Nurturing souls who seek deeper truth,

Fostering growth, igniting the fire,

Empowering seekers to unveil their youth.

With wisdom long hidden, they share their grace,

Reviving the spirit's forgotten refrain,

Proclaiming new knowledge for every race,

Enriching the heart, easing the pain.

In unity with existence's grand design,

They weave threads of insight through darkness and strife,

Encouraging all to embrace the divine,

As prophets awaken the spirit of life.

THOUGHTS

In the quiet, thoughts drift like leaves,

Whispers of the mind, soft as sighs,

They dance on currents, fleeting, free,

A gentle stream, where silence lies.

Pause to witness, let them flow,

Like clouds in a vast, open sky,

No need to grasp or hold them tight,

Just watch them pass, and let them fly.

In this stillness, clarity blooms,

A garden of calm, where worries cease,

With every thought that drifts away,

We find a moment, a breath of peace.

GIFTED WITH EVOLUTION

Rebirth belongs to the immortal spirit alone,

A force of creation, in each heart it's sown,

This spirit, a fragment of the vast, divine scheme,

Embodies the power where life meets the dream.

An energy unfolding, with purpose it flows,

Crafted by Creation, where true potential grows,

A form that evolves through love and through light,

Seeking knowledge and wisdom, embracing the night.

In its journey through time, the spirit ascends,

Maturing through trials, where the heart transcends,

Gifted with evolution, a path to align,

To merge with Creation, where all souls entwine.

As unity beckons, the spirit will soar,

In oneness with essence, forevermore,

For rebirth is not just a cycle to keep,

But a sacred return, where the soul wakes from sleep.

LIFE

Live in freedom, where love and peace intertwine,

Among kindred spirits and all of Creation's grace,

In harmony's embrace, let your heart brightly shine,

Together we flourish, in this shared, sacred space.

Seek joy in Creation, in its many forms,

Embrace the beauty found both near and afar,

No matter the tempests or shifting norms,

Every moment reveals life's guiding star.

Honor yourself with love in thought and deed,

Accept each feeling and dream that you chase,

Through life's trials and triumphs, plant kindness as seed,

In the journey ahead, find your own sacred place.

Though chaos surrounds and shadows may fall,

Remember the beauty that life can bestow,

In each fleeting moment, hear the heart's call,

Life is a treasure, full of wonders to know.

Self- love

Practice self-discipline with gentle care,
For within you lies a strength, unique and true,
Embrace your journey, the path you prepare,
In kindness to yourself, let compassion imbue.
Recognize your worth as an independent soul,
A tender heart deserving of love's replace,
In moments of struggle, let kindness console,
Nurturing the spirit in life's endless race.
Balance your efforts with patience and grace,
For growth flourishes where self-love prevails,
In every challenge, find a sacred space,
To honor your journey as each dream sets sail.
Treat yourself as you would a cherished friend,
With understanding and warmth in every stride,
For in this union, your spirit will mend,
And through self-kindness, true strength will abide.

In Your Hands

If you seek truth and reality's light,

Understand this: you must ignite,

For without your effort, no path will appear,

Help comes from within, not from fear.

You must take pity on your own plight,

To awaken the mind, to broaden the sight.

Only through struggle can wisdom be gained,

And the truths of existence be truly attained.

It's in your hands to unveil what's concealed,

To nurture the intellect, let the heart be revealed.

Through understanding Creation and its ways,

You'll find the path through the fog of your days.

So rise from the shadows, seek and explore,

Embrace the laws that open the door.

For within you lies the power to see,

The deeper truths of what it means to be free.

LOVE

Never doubt the power of sincere love,

For it binds us to all that exists and thrives,

In every spirit and realm, it flows like a dove,

A force that nurtures, as our hearts come alive.

Love is the essence that shapes our fate,

Enduring through trials, it stands strong and true,

Across the ages, in every heart's state,

A beacon of hope, always shining anew.

As the cornerstone of life's grand design,

Love fuels our dreams, urging us to aspire,

To rise to the heights where our souls intertwine,

A flame that ignites our deepest desire.

It pulses forever in harmony's song,

A rhythm unbroken, through joy and through pain,

For love will not falter, it will carry us long,

In the dance of existence, its essence remains.

Do Not Mock

Do not mock those who seek the light,

For their quest for truth is a noble fight.

Your own vision may be narrow and small,

But through their striving, we all stand tall.

In the depths of thought, where values reside,

Expand your horizons, let wisdom be your guide.

Material bounds may cloud your view,

Yet there's richness within that can awaken you.

Embrace the journey of those who explore,

For in their pursuit, there's much to restore.

To find the truth within, to proclaim and to share,

Is a path that can lead us all to care.

So lift each other up in the quest for the real,

For together we grow, and together we heal.

In understanding and compassion, we truly begin,

To uncover the truths that lie deep within.

GROWTH

Be mindful always of your growth anew,

In every realm, let evolution guide,

From personal strides to the depths of view,

Embrace the journey where wisdom resides.

With humble heart, stay focused on your path,

Attend to progress with integrity's light,

For in these shifting times, it's truth that lasts,

A steadfast anchor in the dark of night.

Cultivate a spirit that seeks to learn,

In every moment, find the chance to rise,

Through trials faced, let your inner flame burn,

Awakening insight beneath open skies.

Hold dear the values that shape your core,

For in this quest, your character takes form,

With every lesson, discover more,

As you navigate the tempest and the storm.

LISTEN TO ALL

Allow each voice the space to speak and share,
For all are granted rights to express their mind,
In varied thoughts, a tapestry we wear,
A spectrum rich, where wisdom can be mined.
Listen with care to both the wise and meek,
To every viewpoint, whether bright or dim,
For in the echoes of the strong and weak,
A deeper understanding may begin.
Yet step aside from those who shout and rage,
Avoid the noise that stirs up pointless strife,
For in their clamor, wisdom's often caged,
Their discord may disrupt the peace of life.
Remember still, they're part of the great whole,
Each one a thread in Creation's grand design,
Show respect, though you may not share their goal,
For all humanity is intertwined.

TOGETHER WE RISE

Truth is not held by a single soul,

It flows through existence, making us whole.

In every being, its essence shines bright,

A unity found in the heart of the night.

Indivisible beauty, we cannot sever,

In wholeness we thrive, now and forever.

The fabric of life, woven with care,

Harmony sings in the silence we share.

Each voice a thread in a grand, woven song,

Reflecting the truth where we all belong.

In love and connection, our spirits take flight,

Together we rise, embraced by the light.

So seek the core that binds us in grace,

In the heart of truth, we find our place.

Together we journey, in dreams we ignite,

In the stream of existence, our future is bright.

EACH LIFE

Allot some time each day to seek the calm,
A gentle pause where thoughts can softly flow,
In stillness, find your heart's own soothing balm,
A space for reflection, where wisdom may grow.
Practice kindness in each connection made,
Yet hold your ground, don't lose your sense of self,
For harmony thrives when boundaries are laid,
Balance your heart, not at the cost of wealth.
Respect your fellow beings, each unique,
In every soul, a story waits to unfold,
Though differences may often seem to speak,
Remember, every heart bears dreams untold.
Cherish the truth that binds us, human thread,
Even those whose ways you may not understand,
In this vast tapestry, all are led,
Each life a precious part of Creation's hand.

THE CORE ESSENCE

Pay heed to love, the essence of our core,

A radiant force woven through all we are,

In its gentle glow, life opens each door,

Connecting our spirits, guiding us far.

Welcome the peace that nurtures our dreams,

A refuge where growth and joy intertwine,

In quiet moments, hope softly redeems,

A sanctuary where our hearts align.

Seek harmony, where balance finds its place,

In thoughts and in deeds, let understanding reign,

For every feeling finds its rightful space,

In the tapestry of life, woven without strain.

Do not yield to the rush of the day,

Remain steadfast amid the chaos and clamor,

In tranquility's grasp, let your spirit sway,

Discovering love, the world's greatest glamour.

TRUTH

Truth stands immortal, like creation's design,

Eternal and timeless, a beacon that shines.

Fully developed, it calls to our core,

Worthy of effort, a path to explore.

In its embrace, deception fades away,

Guiding our spirits through night into day.

Investing our will, we rise and we grow,

With truth as our anchor, our essence will flow.

It holds all our energies, our heart's pure intent,

A compass of clarity, where love is well spent.

In seeking the real, we open our eyes,

To the beauty and wisdom that never disguise.

So let us pursue this unwavering light,

In the depths of existence, where wrong turns to right.

For in the circle of what's genuine and true,

We find our own purpose, our spirits renewed.

LIES WITHIN

Within each human, a kingdom of spirit resides,

Yet hidden beneath, where material thought hides.

Obscured by the shadows of doubts and mistakes,

By limits and burdens, the heart often aches.

Erroneous notions and unclaimed potential,

Cover the wisdom that's truly essential.

For knowledge neglected can lead us astray,

But truth is the light that will show us the way.

Through recognition, we peel back the layers,

Transforming our struggles into conscious prayers.

In accepting the truth, we break free from chains,

Unfolding our spirit as love's presence gains.

So let us awaken to what lies within,

Releasing the darkness where light can begin.

In the heart's true expansion, we find our true grace,

Adopting the journey, our rightful place.

BENEATH THE SURFACE

When a human perceives only the outer shell,

Focusing on form, where appearances dwell,

The essence is missed, the spirit concealed,

In the shapes that we see, the heart is revealed.

Yet with eyes of awareness, the deeper truth shines,

Recognizing the spark that in each being aligns.

This consciousness present, though often ignored,

Connects us in unity, a bond to be explored.

For beneath every surface, a light softly glows,

A shared understanding that quietly flows.

In each heart resides a witness so bright,

Guiding us gently through darkness to light.

Embrace this connection, let love redefine,

The way that we see, with a vision divine.

In knowing each other, we nurture our grace,

Building a world where compassion finds space.

IN EVERYTHING

A human being who walks in truth's light,

Sees creation's essence in day and in night.

In every thought, in each action's flow,

The spirit of life in all beings does show.

In nature's embrace, the rhythms are clear,

In every creature and breeze, the sacred is near.

From the smallest of moments to vast cosmic signs,

The threads of existence weave wisdom that shines.

Recognizing the dance in all that we see,

The beauty in chaos, the truth that sets free.

In the heart of each being, a spark of the whole,

Reflects the connection that nurtures the soul.

So live in alignment with the laws that uplift,

For in this awareness, you discover the gift.

In the journey of life, let your spirit take flight,

Clutching the wonder that glimmers in light.

Multiverse

The universe seen is but one of the whole,

A myriad of realms where mysteries unfold.

Within each vast expanse, wonders intertwine,

Universes within, in an infinite line.

Above and below, in layers they thrive,

Each universe vibrant, forever alive.

Beyond what we know, they spiral and soar,

In this grand design, the heart seeks to explore.

Humanity shares in this powerful grace,

Connected to creation, in a sacred space.

For within each being, a fragment resides,

A spark of the spirit where true wisdom abides.

This essence of life, a luminous thread,

Guides us through darkness, where dreams are bred.

In the depths of existence, we find our true role,

Part of the whole, in the dance of the soul.

LOVE AND WISDOM

Love and wisdom, mixed as one,

In the heart of creation, their journey begun.

For in every law that the universe weaves,

Lies the essence of love, where the spirit lives.

Creation's pulse beats with a rhythmic dance,

Each moment a lesson, a dance of grace.

In the fabric of life, their harmony flows,

Binding together the truths that we know.

Wisdom unfolds through compassion and care,

In the depths of our being, love lingers there.

A guiding light shining in shadows and strife,

Illuminating paths in the journey of life.

So cherish this union, this sacred design,

For in love and wisdom, our souls combine.

In the grand tapestry of all that we seek,

They echo the truth, both tender and deep.

ETERNAL TRUTH

Eternal truth stands steadfast and bold,

Unfazed by the shifts that time may unfold.

Its laws are unchanging, a constant refrain,

Timeless and sure, through joy and through pain.

No need for revisions, no need for disguise,

It shines through the ages, a beacon that lies

Beyond fleeting moments, beyond worldly strife,

An unwavering compass, a guide through our life.

Through tempests and trials, its essence remains,

Unmoved by the tides, unshaken by chains.

For truth is a foundation, solid and free,

A treasure unyielding, our path to be.

In the dance of existence, where chaos may reign,

The eternal truth whispers, a soothing refrain.

In every heart's journey, its wisdom is found,

A constant reminder, forever profound.

Forever Young

Eighty years past, youth held the sway,
A spirit untouched by the passage of day.
For the body may falter, grow weary and frail,
Yet the essence within will forever prevail.
In the depths of the heart, the spirit stays bright,
Unbound by the years, it dances in light.
Age is but fleeting, like worries and pain,
A passing shadow, like sun through the rain.
Childhood and youth, like whispers, they fade,
But the truth of our being, in silence, is laid.
External conditions, like leaves in the breeze,
Come and go gently, like clouds through the trees.
What endures is the spirit, its wisdom and grace,
A timeless existence, no age can erase.
In the vastness of being, our essence shines clear,
For the spirit is ageless, forever sincere.

HAPPINESS

Happiness arises from deep within,

A light of creation, where joy can begin.

Not a place to arrive, nor a path to pursue,

But a state of the heart, ever fresh and true.

From the core of our being, joy finds its way,

Rooted in balance, in the dawn of each day.

A harmony woven from spirit and mind,

In stillness and presence, our peace we will find.

Each moment reveals what our thoughts can create,

As we shape our own worlds, it's never too late.

In the quiet, we gather the essence we seek,

For joy is a whisper, both gentle and sweet.

So cherish the spark that ignites from within,

For happiness flourishes where love and hope begin.

In the dance of existence, let your spirit soar,

For true joy is a journey, forever to explore.

BELIEF

In shadows deep, all humankind resides,
A web of doubt where courage often hides.
Belief, a murky shroud, obscures the light,
Choking free thought, extinguishing the fight.
The darkened veil of faith in false divine
Swamps clarity, where wisdom should align.
Tin gods and phantoms whisper empty lies,
Silencing the truth beneath their guise.
In this thick mire, no healthy thought can rise,
Each spark of insight lost, muffled by sighs.
The impulse for discovery fades away,
As recognition of the light turns gray.
Awake, ye souls, and break this binding chain,
Tear through the fog, let clarity remain.
For only then can future pathways gleam,
Emerging from the depths of waking dream.

CREATION

Since the dawn of time's first breath,

Creation shaped its sacred forms,

Where pure spirits gather, free from death,

Igniting evolution's vibrant norms.

In collectives, conscious and aware,

These spirits weave a tapestry bright,

Bound by love, wisdom laid bare,

They shine together, a unified light.

From their depths, new life begins to rise,

Each impulse drawn from their shared grace,

Guided by knowledge that never lies,

In every heart, they find their place.

Lower realms seek the sparks they send,

Nurtured by love, in every soul's flight,

In this divine circle, all paths blend,

Fostering growth through the endless night.

SEVEN

In realms where spirits softly tread,

Seven levels rise, a silent sea,

Each one a thread in the cosmic web,

Reflecting the depths of being's plea.

Creation's pulse in sacred space,

Where light and shadow intertwine,

Spirits dwell in their rightful place,

In the afterlife's eternal design.

Through the layers, they gently glide,

Each journey marked by its own song,

In unity and yet apart,

They navigate where they belong.

Bound by the essence of existence pure,

In the weave of time, they find their way,

A dance of souls, both rich and sure,

In the spirit's realm, forever they stay.

RELEARN

One must embrace the laws of life with care,
And honor them as guiding lights,
Not dwell in pages of ancient creed,
But seek the truth that wisdom invites.
Though many may react with fervent ire,
Beliefs can blind us to what's clear,
The journey asks for open hearts and minds,
To question deeply and persevere.
Divinity shifts in meaning as we grow,
Not bound to texts that once were read,
It lives within the choices that we make,
In the love we share and the lives we lead.
So let us rise above old constraints,
With courage to explore what lies ahead,
For in the quest for understanding's light,
We forge our paths, where truth is spread.

LIFE PURPOSE

The purpose of being on this Earth,

Is to grow in knowledge, love, and grace,

To evolve in harmony with the world,

Finding balance in each sacred space.

Yet, this journey demands a true resolve,

To wield one's power with wisdom and care,

For only through embracing one's own truth,

Can the spirit flourish and deeply share.

In the quest for understanding and light,

Let love guide every step we take,

As we learn to nurture both self and others,

Creating bonds that will never break.

So strive to be knowing and kind,

Harmonizing heart with mind's intent,

For in this dance of growth and love,

We find the meaning in life's true descent.

EACH

Each person must strive to shape their life,

Molding knowledge, love, and true delight,

Harnessing their wisdom and capabilities,

To walk a path that brings forth light.

With every step, let evolution guide,

As justice and humanity take their stand,

For in the growth of self and others,

A kinder world can be crafted by hand.

True happiness blooms when shared with grace,

As we uplift those who walk beside,

Supporting one another in life's great quest,

Creating bonds where compassion can abide.

So let your journey reflect your highest aim,

To lead with love and wisdom's glow,

In nurturing both self and fellow beings,

You sow the seeds of a world we long to know.

THE SELF WITHIN

Each person's focus should turn within,

To nurture their character and soul,

Attending to virtues, thoughts, and deeds,

Aligning life to make them whole.

With careful attention to inner peace,

They shape their path with mindful ease,

Avoiding the traps of fleeting goals,

That lead to beliefs with no grounding there.

Let the heart guide choices, pure and true,

Finding strength in the self that strives,

For genuine fulfillment lies in peace,

Where authenticity truly thrives.

So seek the real, and let go of the false,

Embrace the journey with an open heart,

In paying attention to the self within,

You craft a life where purpose plays its part.

NOT SOLELY FROM AFRICA

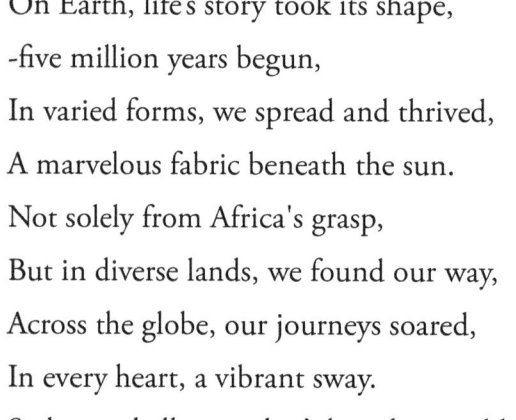

On Earth, life's story took its shape,

-five million years begun,

In varied forms, we spread and thrived,

A marvelous fabric beneath the sun.

Not solely from Africa's grasp,

But in diverse lands, we found our way,

Across the globe, our journeys soared,

In every heart, a vibrant sway.

So let us challenge what's long been told,

And seek the truths that time obscures,

For in the dance of life's embrace,

New narratives of hope endure.

Inner Quest

No soul will find the truth they seek,

By yielding to beliefs alone,

For years may pass in restless search,

Yet still, the heart feels all unknown.

True understanding calls for more,

A journey deep within the mind,

With logic as a guiding light,

And reason's clarity to find.

In self-exploration lies the key,

To recognize the facts that dwell,

For only through this inner quest,

Can one unlock their truth to tell.

So live by insights gleaned through thought,

And weave them into life's own thread,

For in this striving, purpose grows,

And meaning blossoms where you tread.

THE UNITY THAT HELPS US FLOW

Each person must acknowledge the truth,

That minds differ in profound ways,

No two are equal in their insight,

Yet each has value in life's vast maze.

This truth demands a gentle heart,

For none should be seen as lesser or blind,

In the spectrum of human experience,

Respect for each journey is what we find.

Beliefs may diverge, shaped by faith or creed,

But all are woven in nature's design,

In the quest for meaning and understanding,

Each spirit seeks wisdom, each soul will shine.

So embrace the paths that others walk,

With compassion for all who learn and grow,

For in our shared journey through life's vast expanse,

We discover the unity that helps us flow.

RESIST

Everyone must craft their own true way,

Embrace the self that's deep within,

With vivid experiences as their guide,

A journey where authentic lives begin.

Never let another's will confine,

Resist the chains that seek to bind,

For freedom thrives in thoughts and feelings,

In choices made with an open mind.

Stand firm in views that shape your path,

Let opinions bloom like flowers bright,

In every deed, let courage lead,

As you navigate both day and night.

So guard your spirit, cherish your voice,

For in this dance of life, you're free,

With heart and mind in harmony,

You forge your fate, uniquely and boldly.

TO BE INSPIRED

In conversations, choose your themes,

Avoid the shallow, the mundane spree,

Instead, seek topics that inspire,

Where depth and purpose intertwine free.

Let your words carry weight and truth,

Explore ideas that lift the mind,

For in the sharing of what matters,

A richer bond is sure to bind.

So speak of values, insights deep,

Invite the wisdom that lights the way,

For in such dialogue, we truly connect,

And forge a path that leads to brighter days.

Pursue Less

When faced with things that feel askew,
Resist the urge to force their fit,
For in the struggle, peace can fade,
And harmony's lost in anxious grit.
Embrace the wisdom of letting go,
Not all that glimmers must be sought,
In stillness, find what truly serves,
For value lies in what is wrought.
So trust the flow, let nature guide,
In gentle grace, find your own way,
For not all paths must be pursued,
And peace will flourish where you stay.

HUMILITY

In every deed and whispered thought,

Let modesty be your guiding star,

For in humility's gentle touch,

You'll find true strength, both near and far.

In actions small, in words that flow,

A humble heart knows how to grow,

With kindness wrapped in quiet grace,

Your spirit shines, a sacred space.

So tread with care, let ego wane,

In simple truths, let love remain,

For modesty, in all you do,

Brings forth a light that's pure and true.

SAY LESS

In gatherings where many speak,
Be cautious with the words you share,
For in the din, the heart grows weak,
And meaning fades in crowded air.
Voices rise, but clarity dims,
As thoughts entwine and senses blur,
A gentle hush can spark the gems,
While noise obscures what's true and sure.
So linger in the quiet space,
Where silence weaves its subtle thread,
In mindful pauses, find your grace,
For often less is more unsaid.

FORESEEN

In nature's laws, where truths reveal,

Science unfolds, a grand ideal.

Through life's events, we learn to see,

Patterns of the past shaping what will be.

One moment joins another in a rhythmic flow,

A simple sum of instances, wisdom starts to grow.

Like echoes through the ages, predictions take their place,

In the fabric of existence, we find a trace of grace.

So let us glean from every hour,

The lessons wrapped in life's great power.

For in the weave of time, as we observe and learn,

The future whispers softly, urging us to yearn.

STILLNESS

Master the art of longing, yet remain,

Unfettered by the chains that bring you pain.

Desire's flicker dances, bright but tame,

Learn to walk with it, without the flame.

Contemplate the world, let thoughts arise,

Yet shield your mind from their relentless ties.

In quiet reflection, let wisdom flow,

As clarity reveals what we must know.

In every task, embrace a neutral stance,

Approach with calm, allow the heart to dance.

Release the burdens of your hopes and fears,

In balance find the joy that perseveres.

Thus, tread the path of peace, both strong and free,

With open heart and spirit, let it be.

In the stillness of your soul, let calm abide,

Master the art of living, arms spread wide.

REBIRTH

To grow the spirit toward perfection's light,
One lifetime's not enough to reach the goal.
It takes the echoes of a million nights,
Rebirths unfolding through the endless scroll.
For freedom from the flesh, a lengthy quest,
Sixty million years or more to rise,
Beyond the earthly bounds, the spirit's rest,
In realms where form transcends the earthly ties.
Misguided notions claim we change our place,
Reincarnating as a beast or stone.
Yet humans bear a spark that's meant to chase
The path of wisdom, ever seeking home.
Animals cannot tread where humans strive,
Their spirit's aim is bound by earthly grace.
For in our hearts, the quest to know survives,
A journey set in time, a sacred space.

SEE ONE ANOTHER

Recognize the struggle shared by all,

The pain that binds us in our human plight.

To see each other's burdens, hear the call,

Is where a responsible life ignites.

Without this truth, we're lost in endless strife,

A savage battle fought with bitter words.

Our differences breed conflict, clouding life,

As hope for peace becomes a distant bird.

In unity, we find the strength to heal,

A common thread that weaves through every heart.

Embrace the pain, for empathy can feel,

And from this bond, a brighter world can start.

So let us bridge the chasms built by fear,

And recognize the struggle as our own.

In understanding, light will soon appear,

As we transform the darkness we have sown.

THE WISE

The wise stand quiet, letting others speak,
While those of lesser thought chase fleeting words.
Their echoes fill the air, but truth is weak,
As minds untrained believe what they have heard.
A throng of voices, shallow in their claim,
Blindly follow, swayed by fervent cries.
In search of certainty, they play the game,
While deeper insights fade beneath the lies.
They gather close, united by their doubt,
In shadows cast by louder, hollow sounds.
Reason's spark is dimmed, the path is clouded,
As wisdom waits, unseen, in silent bounds.
Yet in the stillness lies a strength profound,
For truth endures when clamor fades away.
The wise, though quiet, nurture thought unbound,
And in the silence, light will find its way.

New Beginnings And Ends

Every journey we take must find its close,

A moment when footsteps can wander no more.

Yet from that stillness, a new spirit grows,

Ready to venture where others explored.

A fresh heart steps forth, driven by dreams,

Reviving the land where old echoes lie.

With renewed purpose, they carve through the seams,

Transforming the path as they reach for the sky.

In the weave of beginnings and ends, we find a place,

Each conclusion sparks light for the next to unfold.

For every end carries beauty in space,

As new stories blossom, brave and bold.

LIFE DANCES

Life dances on the edge of verse and woe,

Each moment a stanza, a tale to unfold,

We weave joy and sorrow, a delicate flow,

In every heartbeat, stories yet untold.

The beauty of laughter mingles with tears,

Echoes of dreams that flicker and fade,

In the mosaic of hopes and fears,

We find the love in the paths we've laid.

So let us embrace this bittersweet art,

For in the struggle, our spirits ignite,

Life's poetry lies deep within the heart,

In the balance of darkness and radiant light.

CREATION

Creation, the Universal consciousness,

authored a tome and it's titled "Nature."

Within its pages lie the enigmatic truths and secrets of life.

A benevolent creator would not pen a text exclusive to a select few.

The great majority of Earth people

were illiterate 2000 years ago.

The truth is, the Bible was written by individuals,

fellow human beings,

seeking solely to exert control over others.

Water is fluid, soft, and yielding.

But water will wear away rock,

which is rigid and cannot yield.

As a rule, whatever is fluid, soft, and yielding

will overcome whatever is rigid and hard.

This serves as a mere illustration

of the profound wisdom that can be gleaned

just by observing the natural world alone.

THE SPIRIT OF ATLANTIS AND MU

Greater Atlantis and Mu, crumbled by strife,

Betrayed by the shadows that darkened their fate,

Few found survival amid the sharp knife,

While the wise took to ships, escaping the hate.

In the ruins of empires, some fell to despair,

Bound into servitude, lost in the fray,

Yet the brilliant took flight, with knowledge to share,

Returning to home worlds, where hope lit the way.

Through the vastness of space, their journeys began,

Guardians of wisdom from ages long gone,

In the silence of stars, they forged a new plan,

Resilient and fierce, their legacy drawn.

From ashes and turmoil, new futures arise,

As echoes of greatness still whisper through night,

In the heart of the cosmos, beneath endless skies,

shines bright.

THE SOL SYSTEM

Beyond the Milky Way, the Sol-system drifts,

A solitary enclave in the cosmic sea,

Floating apart, where the dark silence lifts,

An island of stars, wild and free.

Thirty-five thousand light-years to the core,

To the heart of the galaxy, where secrets lie,

While the Nisan system waits, distant and more,

Seventy-nine thousand light-years in the sky.

On the far edge of spiral arms' embrace,

Where celestial wonders quietly unfold,

A realm where galaxies find their place,

In the universe's dance, timeless and bold.

In this expanse, mysteries weave and blend,

Echoes of creation in the dark's gentle sigh,

A mosaic of light, where boundaries bend,

In the solitude of space, where dreams can fly.

IN THOUGHTS AND DREAMS

Eveyone is a vessel, a seed of might,

With powers waiting, yearning to ignite.

It's our calling to nurture and unfold,

To let the essence of our spirits be bold.

In thoughts and dreams, new realms appear,

Capabilities blossom, pushing past fear.

With every discovery, we venture wide,

Unraveling secrets that within us reside.

Embrace the journey, let curiosity lead,

In the depths of the mind, new ideas breed.

Through trials we grow, and wisdom we gain,

A fabric woven from joy and from pain.

So let your gifts flourish, reach for the skies,

In the dance of creation, let your spirit rise.

For in the hands of humankind lies,

The power to shape worlds, where possibility flies.

BILLY MEIER

In whispers of the cosmic night, he stands,

Billy Meier, jewel of the vast expanse,

From distant worlds, they traverse time's sands,

To learn from him, the goblet of the glance.

The oldest sage with wisdom profound,

A keeper of secrets the universe holds,

Yet Earthlings walk, in shadows unbound,

Blind to the truths that his spirit unfolds.

Through ages, names in cycles repeat,

Henock, Jeremiah, Isaiah, Mohammed and Jmmanuel's grace,

Galileo, Mozart, Socrates, Aristotle, Rasputin wisdom's heartbeat,

Each life a chapter, a familiar face.

Yet still, the world spins, unaware and blind,

Of the light that he carries, the knowledge untold,

In his essence, a universe intertwined,

A legacy rich, as the cosmos unfold.

ETERNAL FIRE

A third-degree burn, a tragic fate,

Destroys the skin, deep layers laid bare,

Muscles beneath, in silence they wait,

Yet pain is absent, a paradox rare.

The surface charred, but numbness remains,

Where once was sensation, now only a void,

In the depths of suffering, an echo of chains,

Yet in this destruction, pain is devoid.

If hell were a place where torment resides,

This burn would defy its fiery decree,

For in the worst wounds, no agony hides,

A silence that whispers, "What can it be?"

So perhaps no inferno can truly exist,

Where pain cannot pierce, where the heart feels none,

In the ashes of anguish, a curious twist,

Revealing the solace when all's said and done.

MY FELLOW BEINGS

To all my fellow beings, lend an ear,

Respect each voice, let kindness take its place.

In every word, let understanding steer,

For differing views can foster grace.

Don't take offense at what others share,

Remember, life's not solely yours to claim.

In open hearts, let empathy repair

The bonds that lift us, not the ones that blame.

Cherish the thoughts that challenge what you know,

In every clash, a seed for growth may lie.

Through dialogue, let shared perspectives flow,

Transforming discord into the sky.

Let's strive for peace, hand in hand we stand,

With patience, love, and respect as our guide.

Together we can cultivate this land,

A world where harmony and hope abide.

A JOURNEY WITHIN

In search of balance, the heart finds its core,

A journey within where true self can soar.

Humility blooms, acceptance takes flight,

Loving oneself in the soft, gentle light.

Deep-rooted confidence stands firm and tall,

Unaffected by malice, unshaken by all.

When spiteful words and deceitful schemes

Fade into silence, the spirit redeems.

Evil emotions once raging and wild

Dissolve into peace, like the calm of a child.

Inner serenity becomes the true guide,

A refuge untouched by the world's cruel tide.

Through reason and clarity, this strength is revealed,

In the honesty cherished, the heart is healed.

As balance unfolds and tranquility grows,

The essence of self in pure stillness flows.

BIRTHRIGHTS

Knowledge and might, strength in our hands,

Wisdom that nurtures, like soft desert sands,

Freedom and love, gifts from the divine,

Creational treasures, eternally mine.

These are our birthrights, the essence of grace,

Endless potentials that time can't erase,

In the weave of existence, they rise and they blend,

A legacy timeless, where journeys transcend.

Each heart holds its wisdom, each mind seeks the light,

Strength fuels our passion, igniting the fight,

For freedom inspires the spirit to soar,

While love is the anchor that opens each door.

So let us nurture this inheritance grand,

With knowledge to guide us, united we stand,

For in knowing our power, we fully ignite,

The brilliance within us, our infinite light.

THE HUMAN BRAIN

Within the human mind, where neurons weave their tale,

Lies the brain, the seat where consciousness sets sail.

Impulses stir within, from subconscious deep,

Emerging as ideas the conscious mind will keep.

The brain, a marvel in its processing might,

Gathers thoughts and visions in the dark of night.

Seeking solutions, reflecting, it discerns,

Turning abstract impulses to knowledge it learns.

From material realms, to spiritual expanse,

Impulses journey, in a cosmic dance.

They accumulate, expand, and transform,

In realms unseen, where mysteries swarm.

Ideas, born of logic, traverse the divide,

To realms ethereal, where they reside.

A constant flow, where wisdom finds its way,

From brain to spirit, where it will stay.

So in the labyrinth of neurons, vast and grand,

Consciousness unfolds, as time's shifting sand.

From the material brain to spiritual heights,

The journey of knowledge, in endless flights.

THE PERFECT UNION

In the labyrinth of the mind's design,

Subconscious forces intertwine.

From their depths, knowledge is set free,

Translating impulses for all to see.

Impulses, data, ideas arrayed,

From subconscious depths conveyed.

By consciousness, they're understood,

Transformed into action, for the greater good.

Self-knowledge, hidden deep within,

A puzzle waiting to begin.

Only when consciousness reveals,

Can truths emerge, where darkness conceals.

Ignorance blinds, keeping truths obscured,

Until consciousness, in full accord,

Unveils the triad's harmonious link,

Releasing knowledge, in which we drink.

Consciousness, subconscious, entwine,

Revealing truths, divine.

In this union, wisdom flows,

From subconscious depths, it grows.

THE DREAM

In the quiet depths of my subconscious mind,

Before Billy Meier's teachings ever become mine,

A dream unfolded, vivid and profound,

Where voices whispered from all around.

An assembly vast, faces unknown,

Projected on screens, a message was shown:

"Seeking volunteers for a mission so dire,

To rescue loved ones lost in cosmic mire.

Relinquish your godly might, embrace mortal fray,

Endure the ticking of time, come what may.

Awaken them from slumber deep,

Reactivate souls from eternal sleep."

Years later, Billy Meier's wisdom I found,

Through words and teachings that did astound.

Suddenly, clarity pierced through the night,

Revealing the purpose, shining bright.

Now I grasp why fate brought me near,

To this mission I hold so dear.

Dedicated to awakening souls with might,

In echoes of that dream's guiding light.

THE MESSIAH'S RETURN

Billy Meier, custodian of ancient truths,

Bearer of Creation Energy, ageless and uncouth.

Across the cosmos, his wisdom unfurls,

Guiding humanity with enlightening pearls.

In a universe vast, where time's rivers flow,

He stands as the Plejaren Teacher we know.

His knowledge transcends, profound and deep,

Revealing secrets that wake minds from sleep.

Like Jmmanuel and Mohammed of old,

His teachings inspire, though often untold.

The Messiah's return in a modern guise,

Billy Meier embodies, to open our eyes.

My life's purpose, to herald his name,

Sharing his wisdom, despite doubt or disdain.

In guiding souls to his cosmic embrace,

Fulfillment abounds in this timeless chace.

LET THEM LAUGH

The so called intellectual humans of Earth,
Shocked and disparaged by truths of worth,
They laugh pitifully at explanations deep,
For real logic and thinking, they struggle to keep.
Lacking understanding of fundamental cognitions,
They mock what transcends their limited conditions.
Unable to grasp the essence profound,
They shrug at questions, truth not found.
In their laughter, a revealing of ignorance stark,
Unknowing of wisdom that lights up the dark.
Yet amidst their doubt and dismissive sighs,
Truth shines on, beyond earthly skies.

Your Choice

In the grand fabric of life, your destiny unfolds,

Woven by thoughts and feelings, tales untold.

Through every action, a ripple effect is spun,

Consequences emerge from what's said and done.

Each interaction, a product of your choice,

A testament to will, with every voice.

Decisions carve paths, shaped by intention,

Creating realities, both boon and contention.

What you sow today, in thought and deed,

Becomes the fabric of your future's need.

Destiny manifests, a reflection true,

Of the journey shaped by the choices you pursue.

IN A GODLESS WORLD

In a world where divinity is found within,

No more titles wield power, no throne to ascend,

Gone are the days of clergy and creed,

No more misguidance, no more earthly greed.

Humanity sees itself as the divine,

No more shepherds claiming what's not thine,

No Popes, Ministers, nor Bishops to sway,

No more demands for what others may pay.

Religion fades, replaced by self-awareness clear,

No intermediaries, no more fear,

Where each soul finds its own sacred truth,

In harmony with life, beyond earthly ruth.

GLORY TO CREATION

In the boundless expanse of space and time,
Creation emerges, a mystery profound,
Entwined with Universal Consciousness' mind,
It shapes existence, in spirals unbound.
A double-helix dance, a cosmic ballet,
Egg-shaped, it cradles galaxies and stars,
Pulsating spiritual energies sway,
Within and without, its essence scars.
Creation, the gemüt, psyche's deep hue,
A oneness encompassing all life's spark,
In epochs seven, its cycles accrue,
Awakening and resting in the dark.
No other Creation in its vast reign,
Births universes, galaxies, and skies,
Justice, love, wisdom, its eternal domain,
Infallible spirit, where truth lies.
Spiritual energy, pure and immense,
In wisdom and love, it forever abides,
A dynamic force, in ceaseless pretense,
Guiding evolution, where all life resides.
Glory to Creation, in its cosmic traverse,
Path of nature, fire, and contemplation,
Consciousness omnipresent, a universe,
In Creation's love, eternal elation.

Seek Peace

In the hustle of our daily drive,
When roads converge, tempers collide,
Instead of rage, let empathy thrive,
Seek peace and let the anger subside.
At the bar where tensions flirt and sting,
Amidst the heat, where jealousies cling,
Rather than fists, let humor spring,
Seek peace and diffuse with a wink.
In line for groceries, patience worn thin,
When queue jumpers invite a din,
Silence the urge to scold and chagrin,
Seek peace, let the tranquility win.
In the park's serene and verdant space,
Where hatred's venom seeks its place,
Resist the urge for violence's embrace,
Seek harmony and peace's gentle trace.
Through moments where conflict seems prime,
In every scene, at any time,
Choose the path that echoes sublime,
Seek peace, let harmony chime.
For in the tumult of our daily strife,
Amidst the storms that shape our life,
Let understanding heal the knife,
Always seek peace, and calm the strife.

NEVER STRAY

Each heart holds a goal, a sacred quest,

Strive in virtue, rise to your best,

Compete in deeds that honor the soul,

In goodness' light, make greatness whole.

Unite your strength, together stand,

Achieve the dreams you've planned,

But let your actions always be,

Guided by fairness, truthfully.

For in the quest for glory's gleam,

Beware the lure of selfish scheme,

To walk the path of equity,

Ensures your legacy, just and free.

So in the race for lofty heights,

Let kindness rule, dispel the night,

And never falter, never stray,

From fairness' path, in every way.

In Illusions

Within Creation's boundless frame,

All truths abide, devoid of shame,

Reject the lure of falsehood's snare,

Lest equity and trust you impair.

Craft not within your soul a lie,

For truths of self can mystify,

Unfairness blooms, doubts arise,

In shadows cast by self-devised.

Nurture instead the laws ordained,

Where justice reigns, and truth sustained,

In harmony with nature's course,

Where honesty holds steadfast force.

Those who forge their truth alone,

Stray from fairness, hearts turned to stone,

Becoming doubters, lost and blind,

In illusions of their own design.

TRUTH IN DREAMS

Amidst the rational minds who see,
Truth's teachings clear, like family,
They hold it close, a cherished part,
Recognized as pure in mind and heart.
Yet others dwell in murky shade,
Concealing truth, decisions made,
They knowingly obscure the light,
In ignorance, they stray from right.
For those with insight, wisdom gleams,
Truth stands firm in their dreams,
A beacon bright in life's expanse,
Guiding souls with its gentle dance.
Let reason reign, let falsehood flee,
Embrace the truth, let minds agree,
In clarity and honesty,
Lies the path to harmony.

BILLY'S WORDS RING CLEAR

Behold the prophet, bearer of truth's scroll,

With signs and wonders, his power extolled,

Follow this path, embrace the real,

Or drift in delusions, lost in the unreal.

Reject false teachings, illusions' grasp,

Seek clarity beyond falsehood's clasp,

Walk in equity, justice's plea,

Or falter in unfairness, spirit unfree.

For Billy's words ring clear and bright,

Guiding hearts through truth's endless night,

To stray from this, a path unwise,

Embrace the real, where justice lies.

In his teachings, find life's truest form,

Where fairness blooms, hearts are reborn,

Let not delusion cloud your sight,

Follow truth, in its purest light.

WHERE CREATION'S WORK IN DANCE

Gaze heavenward, where stars ignite,

Seeking gods and tin gods in the night,

Yet they elude, mere brain's delight,

Truth lies deeper, clear and bright.

Turn your eyes to Earth's expanse,

Where Creation's work in dance,

From crawling creatures to birds in flight,

Witness the primal wellspring's might.

Marvel at miracles untold,

In every corner, truth unfold,

In the chronicles of time enrolled,

A book of worth, its secrets bold.

Wait for the prophet, whose word will ring,

Bringing truth that angels sing,

Spirit, life, in harmony they'll bring,

A future where his deeds will cling.

No To Death Penalty

From the primal wellspring's laws divine,

Rise up as peoples, in peace align,

Love, freedom, harmony entwine,

Guardians of values, in life's design.

No punishments shall cause harm or dread,

Life and limb inviolate, it's said,

No torture, death, nor fear of thread,

Separation measures instead.

In your thoughts and feelings, let compassion flow,

Kindness to all life, let your essence show,

Fearless in truth, let your knowledge grow,

Embrace creation's laws, let wisdom sow.

In Truth Cradle

In the footsteps of those who came before,

Their merits weighed against eternity's lore,

You wander paths they once knew well,

Yet tempted by diverging tales to tell.

They question why you turn from truth's embrace,

Having once tread its righteous, steadfast pace,

Stay steadfast on the path you choose,

In east, west, south, and north, let truth diffuse.

From dawn's first light to twilight's gentle hush,

In homage paid, let truth's voice rush,

Through every corner where shadows fall,

Let truth's beacon shine, illuminating all.

So listen closely to truth's gentle call,

In every heartbeat, in each rise and fall,

For those who've passed and those yet to be,

In truth's cradle, find eternity's key.

IN RESPECTFUL DIALOGUE

In the exchange of thoughts and words,

Approach with openness, like gentle birds,

Listen earnestly to voices shared,

Respect their views with kindness bared.

Present your thoughts with calm resolve,

Let truth and facts your words involve,

No need for aggression or disdain,

In respectful dialogue, truths sustain.

Take no offense from others' ways,

For their actions are not your maze,

Control yourself, your peace hold tight,

In every interaction, shine your light.

If tensions rise, with love withdraw,

Keep inner peace as your highest law,

Navigate with serenity's face,

In the currents of each conversational space.

No One Is Yours

Your boyfriend, girlfriend, husband or wife are not yours to own,

In the symphony of hearts, we're not alone,

No ownership holds sway,

For love's tender grace, in its own special way.

Companionship blossoms where respect is the key,

And trust intertwines, setting spirits free.

No chains of possession, no grip of control,

Love thrives in the spaces where dreams freely unfold.

In the garden of togetherness, dreams find their place,

Nurtured by freedom, in love's gentle grace.

Trust builds bridges across distances wide,

A silent melody in hearts that confide.

These pillars of respect, pure and strong,

Are the bedrock of love that lasts long.

So let us cherish this truth, crystal clear,

In the garden of souls, where love is sincere.

Not as possessions, but as hearts intertwined,

In the eternal dance, where love's light shines.

RELIGION AND SPORTS

Where fervor reigns supreme,

Religion and sports converge unseen,

Both arenas where passions ignite,

Where idols rise in adulation's light.

In temples built of concrete and prayer,

Or stadiums vast with fervent air,

Stars of the field and heavens above,

Evoke reverence and endless love.

Mortal feats and divine decree,

Blend in the eyes of devotees,

For worship knows no boundary line,

In realms where gods and players shine.

Yet amid the fervor's swirling tide,

Truth obscured, reality hides,

For in the adulation's veiled domain,

Illusions blur what's clear and plain.

Religion and sports, as one they stand,

Both shaping hearts across the land,

Where gods and idols take their place,

In the human spirit's eternal chase.

PAST LIFE MEMORY

In dimensions where memories softly tread,
Lies the mystery of lives once led.
From royal thrones to streets unnamed,
A soul's journey, untamed, unchained.
Imagine the weight of past's embrace,
Royalty to rags, a stark shift of place.
Would former glory obscure the now,
Or blend with shadows on life's brow?
To live fully here, in this fleeting hour,
Free from the echoes of ancient power.
For memories fade, like morning dew,
Leaving space for the self anew.
In childhood's gaze, a fleeting glance,
Echoes of past lives may dance.
Yet as time weaves its tapestry,
New stories unfold, endlessly.
Different kin, different roles to play,
A fresh script unfolds, day by day.
Each life a chapter, a chance to grow,
Eternal souls in the ebb and flow.
Embrace the journey, embrace the change,
For life's transformation, profound and strange.
In the grand design, a truth unfolds,
Eternal spirits, in myriad folds.

RELIGION

Religion, the strongest drug that reigns supreme,
A potent force that distorts the dream.
Many are addicted, lost in its embrace,
Their minds adrift in an elevated space.
In this constant high, reality slips away,
The world's true face is kept at bay.
Their perceptions clouded, their senses deceived,
In a divine haze, they remain bereaved.
What's real and true is lost from view,
As they chase the comfort of beliefs untrue.
Their lives are tangled in a sacred mirage,
Unaware of the real world's vivid collage.
In this fervent trance, they drift and sway,
Unseeing the truth that fades away.
Caught in a dream of faith's sweet song,
They wander through life where they don't belong.

Everyone Is Beautiful

In every face, a spark of light does gleam,

A sliver of the vast & grand design,

Each soul a thread within the cosmic scheme,

A glimpse of the universal sign.

Within each heart, a gentle glow reveals,

A part of the great consciousness we share,

In every being, beauty softly heals,

A truth beyond the surface we all bear.

If I can reach this truth & sense its grace,

Then others too can find this inner light,

The way to beauty opens in its place,

A path where all can see the world in bright.

For we are fragments of one grand expanse,

Each holding pieces of the cosmic whole,

In seeing beauty, we embrace the chance,

To understand & free the deeper soul.

HIDDEN FACE

In shadows, souls conceal their inner light,

Hiding true selves, emotions wrapped in night.

On this Earth, we wear masks of grandeur's grace,

While beneath the surface, truth we displace.

A world where masks are worn with practiced ease,

And meaning fades with every false belief.

Surprises strike when despair's shadows arise,

Unseen by those who judged with distant eyes.

I too, have fought the silent, aching fight,

Three times I sought the end, though all saw light.

Within my heart, where spiritual teachings dwell,

The struggle for authenticity does swell.

Our quest for truth, through illusion's mist we steer,

Striving for the real, beyond the false veneer.

Though the path is long, & doubts often bind,

Accepting the raw truth of the Creation Energy teachings only leads to inner peace.

A Bouquet

In lands where Earthly beings roam, their selfish hearts take flight,

A zoo's a testament to their need for dominance and might.

Wild creatures, bound in iron bars, beneath their gazes stay,

While humans marvel, lost in wonder, at lives they cage and sway.

A bouquet, plucked from nature's hand, a fleeting burst of cheer,

Its vibrant colors, soft and bright, soon wither and disappear.

Each bloom, a symbol of their touch, its beauty stripped away,

As humans seek in fleeting grace a moment's bright display.

Pets, too, find their place confined, within the human sphere,

A testament to tender hearts, but also chains we steer.

In cozy beds and leashes long, they find their world defined,

By human whims and gentle hands, yet limited and confined.

Thus sing of Earth's own fragile soul, in these creations clear,

Where selfish needs and fleeting joys to nature's truths adhere.

In zoo, bouquet, and cherished pet, the deeper truth is shown,

That in their grasp of all they hold, the self's true face is known.

PEACE

Let peace be given room to breathe,

And help the world a truth retrieve.

The peace sign often misaligned,

Represents death, when life's enshrined.

Reframe the sign, let it uplift,

A gesture strong, a hopeful gift.

Point upward now, with clear intent,

To signify where life is spent.

Let's shift the symbol, change the view,

To one that fosters growth anew.

In every hand, a sign of grace,

To bring a brighter, kinder place.

Welcome this change with hearts sincere,

And let true peace draw ever near.

For in the sign of life we find,

A path to heal and love mankind.

JUDGING

In the rush of life, we often seek
To judge the paths that others tread,
Yet each soul's freedom is unique,
To live their truth, no harm or dread.
As long as no one suffers pain,
Each choice is theirs to freely claim,
The noise of others views and sights
Is fleeting shadows in the night.
What others think, or how they feel,
Should not disrupt the peace you seek,
For freedom lies in being real,
In living true and never weak.
So live your life with open heart,
Let authenticity impart,
In staying true, you'll find your path
And inner peace will surely become a way of life.

GUARD IT

Let no one shatter your serene space,
Defend your peace with steadfast grace.
Let the anger of others simply flow,
While you remain as calm as a shadow.
Embrace the control you hold within,
Let every storm be lost to the wind.
In the turbulence, stay composed,
For inner peace is where you're enclosed.
Stand firm, let worries pass you by,
With gentle strength, let tensions die.
In your heart, find the stillness you seek,
For peace lies where you are unique.
Protect your soul from every dismay,
Allow harshness to drift away.
In your quiet strength, find your way,
And peace will guide you through each day.

THE FUTURE OF MANKIND

Please aloow me to share what I've come to know,

Truths unveiled, as they gently flow.

Yet, what I offer, though truths they be,

Acceptance molds them into belief, you see.

To truly know, delve deep within,

Investigate, discern, where truth begins.

After your own search, clarity will befall,

No longer beliefs, but knowledge standing tall.

The gods of Earth were human beings, from distant spheres,

Mixed with humans across the years.

Called the original sin, this cosmic blend,

DNA altered, from their world to lend.

Limited to a century's span,

Aggression and traits, from their plan.

Modified for war, a legacy we wear,

Shaping us now, in how we fare.

For Christians, Jmmanuel's name was shared,

Teaching truths, beyond what's declared.

Like Mohammed, a mission to impart,

Wisdom of Creation, to heal the heart.

Undoing DNA's extraterrestrial twist,

Becoming true humans, as we persist.

In the Age of Aquarius, knowledge reigns,

Nokodemion's teachings break old chains.

Reincarnating in February's light,

Bringing wisdom, dispelling night.

Billy Meier, today's vessel and guide,

The future of mankind, to explore worldwide.

About The Author

My name is Waid Sainvil, and I consider myself a free thinker. Though born in Haiti, I see myself as a citizen of the world, unbound by borders or dogmas. For me, true free-thinking means embracing reality as it is, accepting its truths through reason and understanding. It's about looking at life without preconceptions and approaching every situation with a clear mind. Free-thinking operates on the principle that humans must critically observe and deeply investigate reality to grasp its truths fully. Only when we've analyzed every detail with clarity and gained real understanding can we say we are free from belief.

Many people think atheism equates to free-thinking, but they're not the same. Atheism rejects religious belief, but it doesn't automatically make someone a free thinker. True free-thinking goes further; it requires a dedicated search for reality's truths, independent of any belief systems, including atheism itself. A free thinker pulls truth directly from reality, not from preconceived notions, faith, or dogma.

Over the years, I've arrived at certain key insights about life, humanity, and our universe. These truths are not things I wish to impose on anyone but rather offer for reflection. Each person must find their own path to belief through personal exploration. Real understanding can only come when someone looks inward and examines things critically for themselves. Simply accepting what we're told isn't enough; true knowledge comes from questioning, investigating, and transforming belief into understanding.

One of the most significant realizations I've had is that the "gods" we've worshiped throughout history were not divine beings but extraterrestrials—humans from other planets who came to Earth and interacted with early humans. This interaction, often referred to as the "original sin," resulted in interbreeding that altered our DNA. This genetic blending shortened human lifespans and introduced aggressive traits into our makeup. These changes were intentional, imposed by these extraterrestrial visitors, and their effects have been felt throughout human history. The violence and conflict we witness today are echoes of these ancient manipulations.

In Christianity, the figure of Jmmanuel, later known as Jesus, was central because his message went beyond traditional religious teachings. His mission, much like that of the prophet Mohammed, was to share the wisdom of Creation and help humanity undo the extraterrestrial changes to our DNA. His teachings offered a path back to our original state, untainted by these cosmic modifications.

As we move into the Age of Aquarius, we are witnessing a rise in knowledge and understanding. This new era represents a break from the ignorance that has long shackled humanity. The teachings of the ancient figure Nokodemion are re-emerging as significant, offering guidance for the awakening of human consciousness. A key part of this awakening is the reversal of the genetic alterations made by extraterrestrials. As we evolve, we are rediscovering our true potential, breaking free from the aggressive traits imposed on us, and reclaiming the original strength and purpose of humanity.

In the present day, Billy Meier plays a crucial role in sharing these ancient truths. His purpose is to guide humanity through this transformative time, helping us navigate the challenges ahead as we move toward a future built on peace, understanding, and enlightenment. He provides the wisdom we need to explore new possibilities and awaken to our full potential.

Atheism, while rejecting the concept of god, is still a belief system in its own right. The word "atheist" comes from the Greek, meaning "without god," and atheists assert that no divine beings exist. Although it's true that no gods govern the universe, atheism remains a belief, just like any other system of thought. It's based on the certainty that supernatural forces don't influence reality, which is still a position rooted in belief.

Free-thinking transcends both atheism and theism. It's not about rejecting or embracing any single belief but about seeking truth through reason and inquiry, wherever that may lead. It's about freeing the mind from all preconceived notions and understanding reality as it truly is.